PERSONS, PAPERS
AND
THINGS

The committee shall have power to examine witnesses under oath and to send for persons, papers and things.

PARLIAMENTARY RESOLUTION
[Old Form

PERSONS, PAPERS

AND

THINGS

Being the Casual Recollections of a
Journalist with Some Flounderings
in Philosophy

PAUL BILKEY

Editor-in-chief, *Montreal Gazette*

THE RYERSON PRESS - TORONTO

Contents

Introduction

To any whom it may
concern I should say in warning that this little book
is not a history, either of a person, that is to say of
myself, or of a period. It consists of some rather
haphazard recollections and, as I fear, superficial
reflections, the former extending over a working lifetime of something over forty years and the latter
prompted by the things that I have done and seen
and heard, what one calls experience. As a further
word of caution I should add that in what I have
written of men and events and of times and places
I have relied almost wholly upon memory. I am
aware that memory is sometimes treacherous but I
am fairly sure that in no important particular—if
importance attaches at all to any of these particulars
—have I gone far astray; and, at any rate, my
natural indolence constrains me to take the easy
way. In a few instances, which will be clearly
apparent to the reader, if any, I have refreshed my
recollections by going back to original sources, but

these ventures into the realm of real labour have been few and far between. The same habitual aversion to effort has resulted in a disorderly production, a fault of which I am fully conscious and for which I can only entreat the pardon of a possibly bewildered peruser.

I entered newspaper work in Toronto early in January, 1896, being then, I think, eighteen years old, and I have been in it without interruption until now. I suppose I shall remain in it as long as I can continue to count upon the indulgence of other people. In forty years—forty-two to be exact—one gets used to a trade or a profession. Authorities are still uncertain as to which of these categories should include the newspaper writer, and I do not expect that they will have reached a conclusion, even a compromise, in what remains of my lifetime. I am not sure whether the reader, still suppositious, will glean anything from what I have written of the romance of this profession or trade, but if he fails to do so it will be because I myself have failed to tell that side of the story. There is no more interesting life, none more rich in changes and surprises, in swiftly moving scenes, in sudden transitions from monotony to high adventure. For one who has covered every kind of newspaper assignment, and I have covered all or nearly all, whether as a city reporter or as a resident correspondent living away from the home office, or as a wandering scribe, there is constant movement, the formation of new associations, temporary or permanent, the facing of new problems. And speed is always the essence of the contract. The newspaperman always has time at his elbow, there is an office "deadline" always before him, and when his work is done by cable, as much of mine has been, time differences seem usually, if not always, to be operating against him. Moreover, the facilities of communication were not in my early days what they are now. Many, many times I have had to rely upon the ability or the good nature, or both, of a telegraph operator in a remote country place, a man or woman wholly inexperienced in the transmission of newspaper copy. When there are three or four or more rival correspondents competing for the favours of such an operator, then priority depends upon resourcefulness and there have been strange stories told of the methods adopted by enterprising reporters to exclude their competitors from the only telegraph service available. Did not one newspaperman in such a situation many years ago put a Bible in the hands of the operator and tell him to go on sending until the dispatch was ready? I never heard what happened to the news editor at the far end, but I have every right to presume that he was saved, as a brand from the burning.

I don't suppose that any man or woman picking up the morning newspaper at breakfast time ever pauses for a moment to think upon what lies back of the printed word. There is an account of, let us say, a railway catastrophe at some distant point, and every essential fact is set forth for his or her matutinal delectation. The reader, with interest divided between the newspaper page and the dish of bacon and eggs, has not the remotest idea how the story got to the newspaper and, in due time, to his front door. Nothing in the report before him tells anything at all of what was in all probability a quick departure from the newspaper office, a long day or night journey by train or automobile, of, perhaps, a midnight arrival at some hamlet, the nearest jumping-off place, the hiring of a horse and buggy— there were such things in my younger days—and a mad drive through the night over unfamiliar roads to the place of the disaster.   Yet all this, or something like it, has happened.   And even when the scene of destruction and death has been reached, the reporter's task has only just begun.   He must get his facts from reluctant officials, from hysterical survivors, from untrustworthy eye-witnesses, and out of what is usually a conflict of testimony he must sift out a true story, one at least sufficiently accurate to safeguard his newspaper from unpleasantness and possible financial loss.   He must then get that story back to the people who sent him.   He must get to a telegraph office or to a telephone, and thirty-five years ago it was not an easy matter to find the first, much less the second, sometimes very late at night and in an unknown territory.   The facilities are better now but there are still difficulties to be overcome, difficulties which are beyond the conception of the man who grudges two cents for his newspaper.

In the chapters that follow there is no fiction masquerading as fact.   I have written of real events and of real people, of places where I have been and of things that I heard and saw.   Fourteen years, or thereabouts, in the Press Gallery at Ottawa brought me into close contact with public men of every known variety, and with men seeking public favour. I took part in sundry elections, both as a correspondent and as a writer of campaign literature, a product which I have always believed and still believe to be wholly and utterly useless. I look back upon my Gallery days with regret, but only because they came to an end. There is no doubt in my mind that a few years in the Ottawa Press Gallery provide any journalist with an invaluable experience. Even the most indifferent—and not many such ever get into the Gallery in the first place—cannot fail to benefit from his environment, from the company of the country's ablest newspaper writers, and from first-hand knowledge of Parliament and the supreme officialdom with which it is hedged about. I do know that I learned more from my perch above the Speaker's Chair, or in the quiet purlieus of the Library, than I had learned at school. But perhaps that was because my educational deficiencies had left large gaps to be filled. I have set down, as will be seen hereafter, an impression rather than a record of the main political events which occurred during my fourteen years at Ottawa. There are probably some indiscretions, but I can assure my waiting critic that the half has not been told him. He has had that much kinship with Solomon.

In an effort to recapture some of the political atmosphere of 1903, and again of 1911, I have gone back to the pages of the Toronto *Telegram* and have extracted therefrom some reports and sketches. For permission to do this I have to thank my old friend and sometime mentor, Mr. C. O. Knowles, Managing-Editor of the *Telegram*. I have also to thank Mr. H. A. Gwynne for permission to reproduce the correspondence which passed between us in 1916, when, as Editor of the London *Morning Post*, he concerned himself actively with the progress and welfare of the Canadian Expeditionary Force. As an old war correspondent he was in that mid-war period able to turn aside from great responsibilities and anxieties to indulge in an old-time solicitude for the soldier in the field. As Canadian correspondent of the *Morning Post* I was associated with Mr. Gwynne for twenty-five years and I found his friendship invariably helpful. To the eminent author, Mr. John Murray Gibbon, I am deeply indebted for advice and assistance given to me during the later stages of the preparation of this book. Whether or not I should say a word or two of thanks to my daughter, Margaret, seems debatable. She egged and goaded me on to this venture and most of the drudgery has been done by her. It is her book, and for her sake I could wish it were a better one.

1
Preliminary Odds and Ends

THE FRIENDLY spirit so essential to the favourable commencement of any series of personal admissions has been marred by a somewhat protracted and acrimonious discussion between my critical amanuensis and myself whether I should refer, however discreetly, to the matter of my birth. I tell her that any attempt to deceive the reader would be futile, that it is as well to face facts and that, in any event, being born is not unusual. It has happened to others and, although in my case the time and place are largely matters of hearsay, I have this information upon what I consider to be thoroughly dependable authority. I am permitted to mention, therefore, that I was born at St. Georges, Bermuda, in a house called the Fifth Fort, hard by the place where the great heart of

1

that doughty sailor, Sir George Somers, lies buried. Somers it was who effected the first settlement in these islands which, for a time, bore his name. The body of him they took away to rest at last in English earth; but his heart remained in the country to which he gave his life. Legend has it that he died in an attempt to save his colonists from Yellow Jack. The Fifth Fort, by the way—legend again— was built by a gentleman who was sent out from England to erect five forts for the defence of the islands. He finished four and, with the remaining material, constructed a residence for his own use. There he lived and eventually died and they buried him in his garden, which was later, for a brief interval, mine.

I arrived in a January which no Canadian would have recognized as such. For in that Atlantic Paradise in the first month of the year the flowers are in bloom, and bathers cast long shadows over moonlit sands. It is recalled by certain of my relations that my advent synchronized, however fortuitously, with the arrival in the harbour of a sailing ship having in its hold a cargo of nuts, and some undue emphasis has been laid upon this coincidence. Personally, I have always regarded it as wholly irrelevant to the issue.

While still an infant, puling, etc., in my nurse's arms, I was brought to Canada, the immigration laws being somewhat lax in those days. Arriving in Toronto without noise of trumpets or any other of the demonstrations by which alert communities now mark the occurrence of great events, I proceeded to grow up, though to only a limited extent, never having reached even an average altitude.

The Toronto of those days was quite a nice little place, inhabited chiefly by old but impoverished families who, by reason of one of those booms which so often collapse, had been made land-poor. There were horse-cars on the streets for the use of the proletariat, but the aristocratic element still drove about in open carriages driven by magnificent coachmen and drawn by spanking teams, though why spanking, and who did it and why, I could never discover. It was, as I have said, a nice, little place with nothing much east of the Don River, except a couple of picnic parks, nothing west of Parkdale, except a pleasant lakeshore country, and Bloor Street was practically a country road. Seaton Village, Eglinton and Brockton still had places on the map and still had their old inns with their long, outside water-troughs for horses. The little city had its little military and mercantile aristocracy and Sunday dinner was a solemn ritual.

I went to school in Toronto and endured numerous hardships, being a shy youth and not very good at the three R's. At the old Ryerson School, of which Sam McAllister was principal, I was excellent material for the roughnecks of the place, and enjoyed the distinction of being knocked about by several of the now outstanding citizens of Ontario and other places, men prominent in law, in education, and in commerce, and some of them, for all I know, leaders in the church.

Apart from the fact that a young gentleman of Athenian extraction once brought a live alligator to school and permitted the reptile to waddle into the adjoining classroom, occupied by some of the present mothers and grandmothers of Ontario, I recall little of my public school education. The unexpected advent of this smiling saurian among the unprotected extremities of a lot of bashful maids, was profoundly, and to the rest of us, agreeably sensational, but the corporal consequence was catastrophic. Even the Greek hadn't a name for it.

It was the time of the democracy of the drinking cup. Thirsty citizens who had not given up water as a beverage, could refresh themselves from an iron mug attached by an iron chain to an iron fountain at the corner of the street, and they did so, no matter who or what had just preceded them. I used to drink copiously at these unsanitary oases. The same carefree citizens, or rather their children, patronized the ice-cream vendor of that day who pushed a little cart around the dusty streets and tooted a horn, and no children ever followed a Pied Piper with more alacrity than did we in the wake of this benefactor. For the sum of one cent, which was worth more then than now, we could obtain a little heap of delectable, strongly-flavoured ice cream scooped up in a little tin saucer by the thumb and forefinger of the merchant. We never bothered to look at the thumb, nor at the forefinger, nor to consider their other uses. The little tin saucers were, of course, cleaned, having been rinsed in a receptacle of standing water just as all the other tin saucers had been since early morning. If cleanliness be next to godliness, we were a long, long way from our goal, but you may go to the Waldorf or Biltmore in New York, or to the Ritz in London, or to the Royal York in Toronto, or, if your standard is very high and an invitation is available, to that epicurean Eden, the Mount Royal Club in Montreal, and you will get no ice cream that tastes anything like those little one-cent dishes did. Nor does any potato nowadays even suggest the flavour of those we used to roast in our bonfires on the corner lots of our childhood.

In due course, or perhaps a little later, my family moved to one of those near-by Ontario towns wherein the old United Empire Loyalist stock was making its last stand, a town which was suffering economically and socially from the fact that the Grand Trunk Railway, like a certain Levite, had passed by on the other side. In later years, I believe, another railway, playing the role of Good Samaritan, gave the town a new industry or two, but as this line passed over what was in my time the old swimming hole, just above the mill-pond, I cannot look upon its advent as wholly beneficial.

There was more schooling in M——, which isn't the correct initial, but it was of the off and on kind, chiefly off. On the whole, however, it was agreeable. There was, for example, the moment when the headmaster of the public school, unduly excited over some slight infraction of one of his absurd regulations, seized me violently by the ear. "Hold on!" I yelled. "That," he said, "is what I propose doing."

Then there was the High School where sundry male and female teachers held classes in subjects which I could never understand. The school stood on the brow of a hill back of which was an attractive valley with a little creek running through it, a much more agreeable place than any classroom on a summer afternoon. And, be it known, that those summer afternoons were long and lovely; there is

P.P.T.—2

none such now. Moreover, there was a hole in the
fence and it was the custom of some less earnest and
assiduous students to slip through this aperture,
repair to a shady and secluded spot on the creek
bank, and pass the time in uplifting conversation or
in playing Casino with a pack of grimy cards. On
one of these occasions the science master, bless his
kindly heart, appeared in the vicinity with a botany
class. I think he knew who we were because it was
his alleged habit to stand at one of the upper
windows of the school and follow our irregular exits
with a telescope. But he did not know precisely
where we were, at least not until he was close at
hand. Becoming then aware of our presence in his
immediate neighbourhood, he informed his class
that there was a particularly choice specimen of
Ranunculus acris on the other side of the creek, and
he led them over. He has been dead many years,
but I still respect his memory.

It was about this time that I decided to become a
cook on a government dredge. This resolution
came to me in the course of a summer vacation
when my brother and I were camping on the lakeshore in a rented tent. A downward revision of the
stipulated rental had been effected with the owner of
the tent after he had delivered it, to his great and
blasphemous annoyance, but we hadn't been able
to raise the whole three dollars, so that was approxi-
mately that. I think there was a general election in
prospect and a painstaking government, anxious to
maintain and preserve, if not to extend, the depth
of an unused harbour, had sent a dredge to the
mouth of the creek. We became boon companions
of the crew, particularly the cook, to whom we

loaned *The Admirable Lady Biddy Fane*—an excellent book (the title of which acquired from him an entirely original pronunciation). This courtesy was extended in return for certain substantial civilities, including the bestowal of the best lemon pies I ever tasted or which, I believe, any government ever served on any of its dredges. This cook confided in me the impressive fact that he was in receipt of ninety dollars a month and I determined immediately to cultivate the culinary art and to ascertain the political complexion of the government by which he was employed. It seemed important that I should embrace the principles of that party as affording the surest guarantee of national security and progress. Since that time experience has convinced me that, as expressed in dredging and lemon pies, the principles of opposing political groups are not fundamentally dissimilar.

My one excursion into the field of crime I shall pass over with native modesty. My father was a clergyman and there were schisms in the flock. This is not unusual in Christian communities, but the one in which we lived was, I believe, somewhat exceptional in the virulence of its animosities and the diligence with which they were served. At any rate, when my brother and I had occasion to do a little fishing in the creek on Sunday, we were spotted by one of the enemy scouts and, a little later, were served with summonses by the chief of police, who was also the Force, and made to appear before the magistrate. This august individual was a large and portly person, benign of visage and kind of heart. He imposed the lowest fine possible, which was paid, I fear, with borrowed money, and

then asked very earnestly if we had caught any fish.
When we replied in the negative, he shook his head
sadly and seemed genuinely concerned and
disappointed.

At or about this time an election trial was held
in the Town Hall, with a High Court judge presiding
and eminent counsel from Toronto in attendance.
As my father was one of the witnesses, I conceived
it my duty to absent myself from school, that
afternoon's subjects being particularly distasteful,
and witness the proceedings. The trial was an
expression of dissatisfaction on the part of the side
which had lost narrowly in a notably bitter campaign. I have attended many such trials since then
and have learned a good deal more about them than
was possible at that time, but this one remains in
my memory as a sort of introduction to a sphere of
activity in which I was to spend a good many years
and in which I was to associate with politicians of
both varieties, that is to say, the good and the bad.
The division is not of my making. I have found, as
Stevenson would have found, some bad in the best
of them and quite a lot of good in the worst of them.
Where there is a heart of gold, even with some
alloy, one can condone a foot or two of clay. The
outcome of this particular trial I do not recall; but
I remember that, after my father had given his
testimony, the late D'Alton McCarthy turned to
the Bench and said, "It is by the evidence of such
witnesses as this, ministers of the Gospel, that we
hope to prove our case." As the Pater's evidence
had not struck me as being particularly helpful and
as I knew that he was a little disturbed about it
himself, I failed in full appreciation of this grandilo-

quent comment. Subsequent experience, involving an attendance at a great many trials, civil and criminal, has given me the answer. Good bluffing is as useful in a legal emergency as it is in any other.

My scholastic career was interrupted latterly by a temporary expulsion, due to nothing more reprehensible than a courageous refusal to name the instigators and chief actors who had contributed to a major misdemeanour, in which I was myself slightly implicated. After a brief holiday the difficulty was overcome in some way, but the appetite for academic honours was not what it had been. Never very strong, it disappeared completely. A family friend, occupying a high position in Toronto journalism, laboured under the mistaken idea that I possessed some latent talent as a cartoonist. So, on another January morning, not at all like the one in Bermuda, I passed through the red iron gates of the rectory, climbed into a ramshackle cab from the local livery stable and proceeded to the railway station. It was a cold, dark morning. I was eighteen years old, very reserved and shy, and as doubtful of any undeveloped ability or talent as any of my subsequent employers ever were. But I was endowed with a mulish obstinacy which had its uses.

2

Journalism's Age of Innocence

There is a disconcerting
sense of loneliness in the breast of a very young man
on the threshold of an unknown career. I have
had similar sensations in the crowded streets of
New York, of London and of Paris, on the remote
shores of the Magdalen Islands, in the vast stillness
of the Peace River country, and under the great
stars of the Caribbean, but it was never quite as
acute or subduing as in those first days when the
future, if there was one, seemed to lie beyond an
unscalable Alpine barrier. It is a decided advantage
at such times to be without an alternative. Being
driven by necessity is perhaps as good a substitute
for ambition as human life—after all very much of a
hit-or-miss business—affords; but I have never
believed that this is the fault of the successful

minority, or that the great Persian poet was
altogether correct in disposing of life as an imper-
tinence. If the individual in far too many instances,
probably millions of them in every generation, has
lacked the opportunity to develop his natural
ability, the fault has lain in an education system
operating upon the same principle of standardization
as a boot and shoe factory. Vocational training is
doing something to overcome the evil of scholastic
mass production—or miss production—but it did
nothing for me and the element of luck rather than
the advantages of selective education enabled me to
find a market for the goods I had to sell.

Some people are born to a vocation, some choose
it and others have it thrust upon them. Mine was
thrust. I was not to draw pictures but to equip
myself as some sort of secretary to that spectacular
person, the late Edmund E. Shepherd, at that time
editor of *Saturday Night* and of the old *Evening Star*.
There are still a good many people who remember
"Don" Shepherd. He was a big man with a black
moustache and goatee, wore a wide-brimmed, black
felt hat and was understood to pride himself on his
resemblance to "Buffalo Bill." I never had much
to do with him as I never qualified for secretarial
work, but continued in a profession for which,
temperamentally, under the conditions then existing,
I was totally unfitted.

Toronto had three morning papers and three
evenings. Of the mornings, the *Globe*—still at that
time the Liberal Bible—was outstanding in its field.
Something of the great George Brown tradition still
lingered about it. It was eminently respectable
but had not quite lost the crusading spirit of an

earlier day. With such able writers as J. S. Willison, John Ewan, John Lewis, Sam Wood and others, its political and social leadership was universally acknowledged. Its rival, the Conservative *Mail and Empire*, was so conservative as to be colourless, though its staff included men of distinction. It was, and continued to be, a paper without life, yet it maintained its position as the official Tory organ, Toronto and Ontario being, in federal affairs at any rate, far more pronounced in this Conservative allegiance at that time than now. By far the liveliest morning paper was the *World*, published by W. F. MacLean, a Conservative, but wayward and intractable. Politically one of the loneliest men I ever knew, he made his own bed and did it deliberately with a definite journalistic purpose. He was an extraordinary combination of the visionary and the extremely practical publisher. He made the *World* and there was a very general belief that he unmade it. John Ross Robertson's *Telegram* easily dominated the evening field. As a business enterprise it was remarkably successful, but its editorial policy was peculiar. Its proprietor and its editor were alike in their prejudices, and prejudice and personal preferences were the bases of their policy. The *Telegram* was intensely pro-Orange, anti-French and fanatically anti-clerical. Naturally, it made a very strong appeal to a citizenry whose mind was attuned to just those things. It is more moderate and more tolerant now, possibly because the appetite of its community has changed.

Journalism is not as sober now as it was then, but those engaged in it are much more so. The inebriation has passed from the man to the product. The average daily newspaper forty years ago was not three-fourths full of so-called features, syndicated nonsense, land-water beauties and comic strips which lack the element of comedy. In its news columns as well as its advertising sections it was a much cleaner product than it is now. Still, it is as true of newspapers as it is of groceries that you cannot sell what people do not want, and if there are any survivals of the old journalistic order, they are very few and far between and are probably losing money. Nevertheless, some old-fashioned people may still look back rather wistfully to newspapers which did not create the illusion of being published in a lady's bedroom and in which English grammar still held some lingering respect. Victorian dignity remained a social habit. The great Queen was still comfortably seated upon her broad-based throne and the time had not yet come for literary scavengers to rout among the royal dustbins in search of superfluous proof that she was a woman as well as a queen. Edward the Seventh was yet on his long probation as Prince of Wales. George the Fifth, as Duke of York, was still further from St. Edward's crown, and there was a little boy of two years or thereabouts who was to reign for a short while, uncrowned, as the eighth Edward. Much water was to flow under the bridge, some of it muddy.

In the closing years of the nineteenth century democracy was not rushing to its logical and disastrous destiny with anything like the speed which it has since attained. It was a rather tranquil time when men could sleep o' nights without dreaming of Mussolinis, Hitlers and Stalins, or of what happens when an Oriental race becomes civilized. There were some, even intelligent and discriminating persons, who still clung to the conviction that the clamour of an ignorant, usually covetous, often indolent and always intolerant mob must necessarily be inspired. It has always seemed to me that the proverb, *Vox populi, vox Dei,* is singularly presumptuous and, with all due respect to William of Malmesbury, or whoever it was, the proposition is one to which I cannot subscribe.

. . . . . .

The staff to which I was introduced and of which I became a member was disproportionately composed of accomplished drunkards. After the assignment book was made up in the morning, they repaired to the nearest pub. They pubbed at frequent intervals until three o'clock, or thereabouts, in the afternoon, when the paper came off the press and its competitors arrived. The daily storm then took place, consisting chiefly of a series of editorial bellowings, coupled with defamatory references to those members of the staff who had missed something or other that a rival newspaper had managed to secure. After the storm, the calm; the irate editor and his entire flock, or almost the entire flock, adjourned to an adjacent bar, where a pleasant time was had by all. I am not suggesting that these alcoholic addicts were not otherwise good newspaper men. They were. They were well above the average and some wrote brilliantly, but not many of them survived. Not many of that staff are now living, but some made names for themselves and went far.

I became a police reporter and, as part of my initiation, or perhaps at some later stage, was photographed by the official custodian of the local Rogues' Gallery. This was represented to me as an expression of hospitality though there remains the possibility that an alert and far-seeing police officer was considering future eventualities. Some years later—rather a good many—I was finger-printed in the same friendly spirit at the headquarters of the Dominion Police in Ottawa, so that, between the two, I have had more than the usual inducement to prefer the straight and narrow path at all times when under observation.

I had no particular liking for the arm of the law, long or short. I had less for the kind of people who appeared from day to day in the police court, which was itself a smelly place made partially agreeable only by the presence and personality of that remarkable magistrate, Colonel George Taylor Denison. Inquests were uniformly unpleasant as were also the occasionally necessary inspections of suicides, victims of murder or of accident. Nor did I ever succeed in hardening myself to the easy performance of the task which practically every reporter is called upon to discharge almost every day of his life, namely, that of intruding into the offices of business men or into the homes, often of afflicted people, and asking impertinent and sometimes brutal questions. But it had to be done. One police court association I recall with a great deal of pleasure. I had a fellow reporter, a representative of the Toronto *Globe*, who was different from the rest of us, very different from one who afterwards poisoned himself—unless politics be, as some people think it is, a poison. This *Globe*

man wore striped flannels, carried a large yellow
walking stick, and wrote extensive reports of all
cases involving domestic misery, of which there were
plenty. We called him Rex. He was William
Lyon Mackenzie King, now for the fourth time
Prime Minister of Canada.

As I have hinted, I had not entered this field
with any deeply-rooted affection for policemen,
probably because of the unfortunate issue of the
ill-timed piscatorial adventure, hereinbefore mentioned, and also because during a Hallowe'en
celebration in the town which I had recently left I
had again fallen foul of the Force and been severely
admonished in the matter of, I think, a missing gate.
These experiences had bred in me a lively aversion
to blue uniforms and bright buttons and to all who
wore them.   Despite this unfriendly predisposition,
my years as a police reporter and my long association
with the police of all ranks brought with them
friendships which I have always cherished.   I have
known a policeman to take a drink of hard liquor
surreptitiously in the stationhouse; and I have
known a constable to exchange gurgles with a beer
bottle in an alley under cover of night, but in no
instance that I recall did harm come of these
spirituous indiscretions. One at least of the offenders
rose to high rank, if not the highest, in the Force
and retired with a fine reputation.   There were, of
course, some mean men, small of soul and warped of
outlook, doubtless having come that way from their
cradles, but the majority were capable, loyal, and
completely fearless.   I knew something of the risks
they took in the daily discharge of their duties, of
the narrow escapes they had and of how little they

thought of them. I have in mind a career of unusual distinction which nearly ended on the floor of an old house on St. Patrick's Square when a bullet missed its mark by the fraction of an inch, and it was fired at close range. Courage and quick shooting counted for something in those days, as in the case of the Varcoe murder on Queen Street. The escaping killer was winged by a young constable, plodding what had been up to that moment a monotonous beat, an inconspicuous cog in a big machine. That one shot started him up the ladder and he became Chief of Police. Sometimes, but not often, the boot was on the other foot and the policeman died, as in the case of a county constable, one Boyd, victim of the Rutledge-Rice-Jones trio. But Boyd was avenged.

Rutledge came of a respectable family in a town not far from Toronto. Rice was, I believe, the son of a Michigan farmer, and Jones, if my memory serves me, hailed from New York. They were desperate men, robbers and killers, but, as will be seen hereafter, they paid. After looting a bank in Parkdale they disappeared, leaving the police more or less at sea. Next they robbed a bank at Aurora, stole a horse and drove back to Toronto, hiding over a restaurant in upper Yonge Street. Their identity in some way became known to the police, who watched their retreat from an hotel across the street, but never succeeded in getting all three in the place at one time. While the minions of the law were waiting to make the haul complete, the whole bag escaped, took a boat to Niagara and again disappeared. The Chicago police took them in a rooming-house in that city and were lucky enough to get them in bed and surprise them before they could reach under their pillows, Brought back to Toronto, they were placed on trial at what was then the Court of General Sessions. After their first appearance there they were placed in a cab with two county constables to be driven back to the gaol. Nothing happened until the cab was passing the old General Hospital on Gerrard Street when, at the corner of, I think, Sackville Street, a young man, or a woman disguised as a man—the police were never sure about this—walked up to the vehicle and passed in, or threw in, two forty-five calibre revolvers, which two of the desperadoes seized—the middle one, Jones, was handcuffed to the other two. The constables were ordered to put up their hands. Boyd, an elderly man, being slow about it, was shot through the temple. The men then left the cab and made for a passing street-car, while exchanging shots with the remaining constable. Traces of that barrage may yet be found in the doors of a row of cottages on the south side of the street. The fleeing men got to the street-car and were endeavouring to commandeer it when a passenger pulled the trolley rope; the car stopped and the three were subdued and returned to the gaol.

Jones had been shot through the elbow, the bullet inflicting a peculiar wound, but Rice and Rutledge were unhurt beyond a few cuts and bruises suffered during their recapture. Two of the trio escaped the gallows, but not death. Rutledge leaped from an iron gallery of the gaol and, when I got there, his broken body was still lying on the floor beneath. Later on I went again to that gloomy prison to see the last of Rice, who had been tried and convicted of murder. It was not an agreeable spectacle, but I had little pity for him. He had killed an inoffensive man whom I had known for years. Still later, in the old Trinity Medical School, in a jar in a long row of exhibits, I saw the elbow of Jones and the curious wound that had finished him. I had followed this trio, fortunately at a safe distance, from the beginning to the end, and I tell the story here by way of showing what police reporting was like at that time and what, I suppose, it is like now. There is variety in it and occasionally some risk, and it affords abundant material for anyone who inclines to moralize. Rice was the only man I ever saw hanged, but one of my newspaper colleagues built up his reputation as a recorder of these gruesome exits, while another one, who was by no means of a morbid disposition, possessed a fairly large collection of pieces of rope, each from a noose which had broken some unfortunate's neck. I don't know what became of these sinister souvenirs, but I have never felt poorer through lacking them.

. . . . . .

Among other things, Toronto, in 1896, was becoming what would be called now "transportation-conscious." The new Union Station was in process of completion on Front Street on the block between Bay and Simcoe. It was an expensive structure and evidently suited to the tastes of those who liked to dream they dwelt in marble halls, but to the travelling public it was not so much a dream as a nightmare, an architectural conundrum with the odds against the out-going passenger ever finding his train or the in-coming ever finding the street. It has since been replaced by an almost equally perplexing terminal, but there is this difference, that while the traveller outward-bound experiences comparatively little difficulty, the arriving passenger gets into the city through as complicated a series of stairways and passages as human ingenuity could devise. In other words, it is much easier to get out of Toronto than to get into it and, while there are some who hold this to be, on the whole, beneficial to mankind, it is none the less confusing to the stranger unaccustomed to this curious form of civic reception.

And, while we are still on Front Street, we may recall with a sense of deep bereavement the passing of that most homely and delightful of all Canadian caravanseries, the old Queen's Hotel. There is nothing to be said, of course, against the Royal York which stands there now, the British Empire's biggest and, in many respects, perhaps, its best. But the Queen's was a thing apart, a very charming relic of an older and more peaceful time, a mellow place with an atmosphere of comfort and decorum which the stone monuments of these days can never recapture. It was one of those inns before which Mr. Pickwick could quite properly have alighted from a coach and six, which, after a leisurely exchange of passengers and the quenching of the coachman's thirst, would roll away to the thunder of hoofs and the blaring of the horn along a white and never-ending road. I never go in or out of the Royal York without somehow feeling about me the ghostly presence of the old Queen's on a lazy summer day and the always immaculate Mr. Winnett hovering henlike among his guests.

.   .   .   .

Among my colleagues on the *Evening Star* at
different times were Harvey O'Higgins, who afterwards went to the United States and achieved some
fame as a writer of short stories; H. Addington
Bruce, who also emigrated and became, I believe, a
successful syndicate writer; Harry Gadsby, who was
writing fun and irony then as he is now; Victor Ross,
who ended his life as Vice-President of the Imperial
Oil Company; and W. McC. Davidson, who was a
disciple of Horace Greeley to the extent that he went
west, bought a newspaper in Calgary, prospered
and is now, I am glad to say, living in blissful
retirement.   Also, for a short time, we had with us
Billy Allison, who wrote under the pseudonym of
"John of Gaunt" and is now the Reverend William
Talbot Allison, who recently retired as Professor of
English at the University of Manitoba and was for
many years literary critic of the Winnipeg *Tribune*.
These were not the more bibulous members of the
staff.   All were, as I have said, good fellows and
able men.
    I cannot recall who was the Cataline in this
company, but somebody proposed that on the next
occasion of an editorial onslaught, the victim,
whoever he might be, should retaliate in kind.
Every one agreed, each in the comfortable belief
that the lightning would strike elsewhere.   The
moment came.   The editor orated fluently on the
general incompetence of his subordinates and then,
having in his hand one of the other evening newspapers, fixed a baleful and menacing eye on me.
Bear in mind that I was the youngest and the
greenest.   Out of the corner of my eye I observed
the inexorable judgment of my fellow conspirators

as written in their visages. I knew that if I failed
I would be an outcast and a thing of scorn. Where-
fore and whereupon, with that happy feeling of one
who walks over a precipice, and mentally repeating
the words which Danton probably didn't say to
himself at the steps of the guillotine, I turned upon
the great man and, although handicapped by a
limited vocabulary, I loosed upon him as much
sulphuric invective as I could think of at the
moment.

In making what I considered an adequate
reference to his immediate ancestry, I was obliged to
discard, temporarily, the Darwinian theory.

The experiences of later years have brought me
back to it. After watching politicians and constituents scratching each other's backs and after
listening, for many days and nights, to the gibberish
of parliamentarians (not including those who paid
me to write their speeches for them) and after
observing a number of prime ministers hanging on
to office by their tails, I have been convinced that,
at least, the theory rests upon a foundation of
plausibility. But to return to our muttons. I have
never in my life seen a man so utterly astonished. A
wolf suddenly socked in the nose by a rabbit might
look that way. But it didn't last long. He gazed
around the room and the light of understanding
shone upon his countenance. He laughed—and we
all, with one accord, adjourned across the road.

The *Evening Star*, when I went to it, was shining
rather faintly in the firmament. There were few
such palatial newspaper offices then as there are now.
The *Star* was published from an upper storey of a
narrow building on Yonge Street, the editorial

department being separated from the composing
room by a wooden partition. The *Telegram*, to
which I went a few years later, had its own building
at the south-west corner of King and Bay streets,
opposite the *Mail* building. After John Ross
Robertson erected what was then the last word in
newspaper habitation at Bay and Melinda streets,
the vacated structure became Clancey's Saloon, a
very gorgeous place with highly ornate interior
decorations in what the owner understood to be the
Moorish style. The Bank of Toronto head office
stands there now; indeed, there are very few
survivors of the well-patronized pubs of that period
—the Dog and Duck, Turtle Hall, the Bodega, the
English Chop-House, Morgan's, the Bay Tree, and
the Golden Fleece. All very comforting places,
these, warmly agreeable on a winter evening, havens
to which one could repair and, at a modest outlay,
forget a while man's inhumanity to man and, more
especially, the iniquities of city editors. What has
become of the long mahogany bars, the brass rails,
the mirrors and the clean-shaven priests of Bacchus
who were there, and why were they all clean-
shaven? Was it in unconscious deference to the
ancient maxim that good wine needs no bush?

The *Evening Star* moved to the then *Saturday
Night* building on Adelaide Street and, after lingering
there for a few years, was sold to Mr. Joseph E.
Atkinson. I was immediately discharged and the
Toronto *Daily Star*, unhampered by ethical
restraints, went on its upward way.

For ten years, or thereabouts, I laboured on the
Toronto *Telegram* under John Ross Robertson, who
was a curious mixture of generosity and thrift. He

had a number of qualities in common with Hugh
Graham, later Lord Atholstan, of the Montreal
Star, whom, possibly for that reason, he disliked.
The *Telegram* staff went a very long way in exempli-
fying the proverb that virtue is its own reward; and
yet, oddly enough, a reporter returning from an
out-of-town assignment could not turn in too big an
expense account. This, in a way, expressed the
curious one-sided liberality which was characteristic
of John Ross Robertson. One hand was generous,
but it didn't let the other into the secret.

There was in the offing at this period a youngish
man of serious bent who had served some time on
the *Telegram* and had afterwards entered the
Assessment Department and later the City Solici-
tor's Office as student-at-law. After Robert J.
Fleming, who had been mayor and was "The
People's Bob," became Assessment Commissioner,
he actively took up this youngish man, who could
practise wizardry on any sort of mathematical
rebus. Tom White wore a black coat then, as he
does now. It was his duty to attend the Court of
Revision and there dispute with citizens who sought
assessment reductions. It used to be said that if
these unfortunate burghers, having passed through
the hands of the youngish man, escaped without
having their assessment increased, they were fortunate indeed. Then, one fine day, a group of
capitalists in the vicinity formed the National Trust
Company and put Tom White into it, to become its
Vice-President and General Manager. The Right
Honourable Sir Thomas White, Canada's war-time
Finance Minister, now Chairman of the Board of the
Canadian Bank of Commerce, is a man whose

friendship I have enjoyed for many years, and this notwithstanding the fact that it was he who imposed the income tax. Not many people know that he could have been Prime Minister of Canada had he so willed.

And also, about this time, one Edward Wentworth Beatty, of whom the public was to hear a good deal, was being called to the Bar of Ontario at Osgoode Hall—a *rara avis*, this Edward Beatty, born with a mouthful of silver spoons, in his case surplus and superfluous equipment since his head was full of ideas and, through sheer intellectual force alone, he was destined to reach the heights. It was through no fault of his that those heights upon which a Stephen, a Van Horne and a Shaughnessey had basked in the sunlight of ever-growing prosperity, and from which Lord Shaughnessey and, perhaps to a lesser extent, Sir William Van Horne, had looked down with arrogance upon all competitors, became in his time buffeted and shaken by the storms of adversity. His predecessors had been great railroaders, but Shaughnessey had been a hard man and intolerant, a great mogul in the world of transportation. He had once sold candles in Milwaukee and he had become a baron in the British Empire. He had made the name of the Canadian Pacific Railway and its subsidiary services known throughout the world and the credit of the C.P.R. marched side by side with the credit of the Dominion. But he left behind him a legacy of rancour throughout the Canadian West, a legacy which the railway system and its correlated agencies had perforce to inherit. And thus it happened that when the C.P.R. under Edward Beatty needed friends, stood indeed in desperate need of them, they were not to be found.

Beatty was chosen as Shaughnessey's successor because he had rendered the Company splendid service in its law department and the theory which prevailed was that the problems of the Company thenceforth would be problems of policy and law rather than of construction and operation. As chairman and president, Sir Edward Beatty has done all that a capable executive and a most industrious servant could possibly do, but the cards have all been stacked against him. He has had to compete with a publicly owned and politically operated rival, equipped with something that no privately owned enterprise could ever hope to have, a financial shock-absorber of practically unlimited capacity. The development of highway transportation has of course injured the business of the Canadian National fully as much as it has injured that of the Canadian Pacific, but the Canadian National can watch the diversion of its traffic to the truck and the autobus with complacency; it does not have to make money. The once all-powerful Canadian Pacific, still adhering to its traditionally high standard of service, has no Parliament behind it to pay its bills. By prudent and skilful management it has continued fulfilling its contract with the country, the obligations set forth in its charter, and has remained solvent. But for years its common stockholders, owners of the system, have had no return upon their capital, nor is there any likelihood of a dividend for a considerable time to come. It has been said, and not without truth, that these unfortunate people invested in the good faith of the Dominion and that the reed broke under them.

Sir Edward Beatty is aging prematurely under these conditions, but his mind has always the fine edge of his earlier days. He is one of the friendliest men on earth, although I have sometimes thought his friends and those upon whom he has relied for advice have been badly chosen. I have often heard him criticized for the frequency of his public addresses, and it does seem that for a man with such burdensome industrial responsibilities he speaks too often. This is the usual hasty judgment. The truth is that Sir Edward Beatty is something of a crusader. He sees great opportunities for constructive reform in public affairs and he discharges what he believes to be his duty to his fellow-citizens. I am not referring to his frequent talks on railway matters but to the many other questions that he has raised and suggestions that he has made. It so happens that no one else sees these problems with the same clarity, or, seeing them, has the ability or the sense of civic duty necessary to present his arguments and conclusions to those organized groups of society more closely interested in them. In short, if Sir Edward Beatty talks too much, it is because others think and talk too little.

He is a bachelor, a tremendous worker and knows everything that is going on everywhere. Through his big room over the Windsor Street Station in Montreal pass all sorts of people from all sorts of places, Canadians and strangers from far corners of the world, each contributing his little something of information, each taking away with him some golden counsel.

3

Giants in Those Days?

I‌T MAY only be because I
was a somewhat impressionable youth and had not
the same background of experience then that I have
now, but it has always seemed to me that within
the late nineties the prestige of the Bench and Bar
in Ontario stood higher than it has ever done since
that time. The higher judiciary included such
men as the Chancellor, Sir John Boyd, the monu-
mental Ferguson, Street, whom they called the
hanging judge, Rose and others, great jurists all of
them. At the Bar there were giants; the Blakes,
the Oslers, and the McCarthys; Sam Blake, a great
power in church as well as in law; D'Alton
McCarthy, equally eminent as parliamentarian and
barrister; B. B. Osler, one of a family distinguished
in law, in medicine, and in finance, and perhaps the

greatest master of his day in criminal jurisprudence; Aylesworth, sometime Postmaster-General of Canada and now Senator Sir Allan Aylesworth; George Tait Blackstock—these were some of the others in the front rank. If these men seemed bigger than their successors, it is probably because I was less familiar with their beginnings. Since that time I have seen a great many men achieve judicial preferment through political service but, as that road had been well travelled before, this should not be held against them. Indeed, they have proven to be very able and very conscientious judges.

I have mentioned Blackstock, a man who was in some respects in a class by himself, handsome, cultured, brilliantly clever and with a dangerously deceptive air of indolence. I saw him once at a murder trial in Hamilton, when he was pitted against a young barrister of some football fame and of considerable social prominence locally. Blackstock was prosecuting. The defending counsel put his client in the box and guided him through an examination designed to convince the jury that he was the world's most innocent and inoffensive man. Blackstock, meanwhile, gave no appearance of paying any attention whatever. My recollection is that he was reading a newspaper. But when the time came for cross-examination he got to his feet with an air of utter weariness, drawled perhaps half-a-dozen questions, and the poor wretch in the witness box went on his way to the gallows. Not that young lawyers do not have their day. They do. As in most other vocations, they crawl before they can walk, they learn by trial and error, but the good ones get on, and I can recall the names of many who were juniors between, say, 1896 and 1906, and who are now leaders of their profession and not a few of them are, or have been, judges in the courts of Ontario and Western Canada.

.   .   .   .   .   .

At this point, though there is no particular sequence, it becomes my privilege to cast a revealing light upon the disappearance of Ambrose J. Small, theatre magnate, though I could suggest a better word. I first met this creature when he was in control of the Toronto Opera House and long before he had extended his activities to other theatres and other cities. Every reporter in my young day was obliged to be a theatrical critic off and on. I was sent to the Small theatre to report one of those slap-stick comedies that were common on the so-called legitimate stage when there was one. I suppose the show on this occasion was no lower than the average but, being young and sensitive, relying on my own judgment and being, therefore, ill-advised, I portrayed the performance with an unfortunate fidelity to facts. I did the same thing some years later to a celebrated revivalist in Massey Hall, and there was a terrific row about it, a row which did not subside even when I pointed out that no religious revivalist should quarrel with the truth. There was also a disturbance over this Toronto Opera House business. I was told, politely but firmly, that accuracy in the reporting of theatrical entertainments was sometimes prejudicial to the interests of the advertising department; also that Mr. Ambrose J. Small was both surprised and hurt. The next time I went to the theatre I was shown into a box and, thereafter, Mr. Small and I maintained a relationship of armed cordiality. As to his disappearance on the night of December 2, 1919, after just cashing in for a million dollars or thereabouts, one consideration alone leads inevitably to the conclusion that he was eliminated with premeditated violence. A man like Ambrose J. Small might "walk out on" his relations and friends with a million dollars, but he would never do it without the million.

·   ·   ·   ·   ·   ·

Even in this day and generation, visitors to Toronto from more wayward towns and cities marvel at the Sunday stillness of the place, at the rigid enforcement of restrictive laws, at the general movement of the populace towards the churches in the morning, and at the puritan pride manifested by police officers in prosecuting some lost soul who has sold a shilling's worth of tobacco on this day. Toronto still maintains its moral bulwarks against the so-called continental Sunday, but it has gone a long way in the general direction of the devil since, but not because, I was a youngster in its environs. In those far-off days, Toronto, except at church time, was a place of deserted streets, of unbelievable quiet, of sedate and solemn behaviour, of almost complete idleness even in the home. No games were permitted and in the more carefully governed households only carefully selected books were read. And the curious thing about all this is that those long-ago Sundays seem now to have been on the whole as pleasant as they were placid, as comforting as they were cloistered, as dignified as they were dull. The church bell did not peal in competition with the motor horn or the clanging bell of the street car, nor was the preacher pitted against the broadcast buffoonery of a so-called radio star. There were, of course, no automobiles and no radios and, until close to the turn of the century, there were no Sunday street cars. The Sunday car movement was just gaining headway when I went to the *Evening Star* as a green reporter, and the *Star*, whose then ownership was not, I believe, remote from that of the street railway, was urgently championing a Sunday transportation service. The battle waxed and waned. It was fought with peculiar bitterness and with frequent exchanges of personal invective, as is the case with most divisions of opinion on moral or quasi-moral issues. When the late Sam Blake, pillar of the low church party in the Church of England, uttered his broadsides against the introduction of Sunday labour, he was promptly, and as offensively as possible, reminded that he drove to church in a carriage, that his coachman was as much entitled to Sunday freedom as was a street-car conductor and that a man who could ride about on his own four rubber-tired wheels, luxuriantly cushioned and lap-robed, should not deny his less fortunate fellow being the means of getting about from place to place as a humble strapholder on a jolting street car.

At this period the bicycle was at the zenith of its popularity. People still called it a "safety" to distinguish it from its tall and perilous progenitor, then passing into desuetude. Cycling, whether for business or for pleasure, was general in every walk of life, the messenger boy rubbing knees with the

grave and reverend seigneur soberly wheeling to
and from his counting house. The entire organization of the *Evening Star* was turned out one Sunday
to count the bicycling armies riding countryward,
the idea being to prove that the masses of the people
were yearning for some means of getting about on
the Sabbath day, of making their way to the countryside or to the lakeshores east and west of the city.
I was paired with a gentleman from the mailing-room
and we were stationed at the edge of High Park.
It is in my mind that the tally we made was not
entirely accurate. It was too much like counting
sheep, and the well-known and soporific influence of
the occupation became at times overpowering.
Moreover, my companion, the gentleman from the
mailing-room, manifested a division of interest very
early in the proceedings, preferring to estimate or to
speculate upon the potential frailty of unaccom-
panied maidens passing hither and thither in the
park. The best we could do under these difficult
conditions was to strike an average. We did this
and were able to march into the office on Monday
morning with a conclusive case. I am not sure
that our statistics were wholly instrumental in
turning the tide of public opinion, but the Sunday
cars came. Having gone thus far, however, the
pious burghers of Toronto resolutely set their faces
against any further relaxation of the Sunday code.
For a long time thereafter misguided merchants
were prosecuted for the surreptitious selling of an
occasional five-cent dish of ice cream and it was not
until some persevering pundit of the law discovered
that ice cream was a food that this nefarious
merchandising practice ceased to be a crime.

It was not the custom of respectable Toronto citizens at the commencement of the century to burst into song on the public streets or to sit upon the curbstone in a bibulous exchange of confidence with strangers; yet these things happened on Pretoria night. News of the fall of the Transvaal capital in the early summer of 1900 reached Toronto —a bit prematurely, I think—when evening was well advanced, and produced one of the most extraordinary demonstrations of popular rejoicing that I have ever witnessed. I was attending an inquest at the Emergency Hospital, which stood on Bay Street on or near the site of the present National Club. There was an immediate and general exodus; the entire court, coroner, counsel, jurymen, witnesses, etc., left the building—and the corpse—to join the throngs that were already engaging in the manufacture of what in these days is called "whoopee." In half an hour's time the downtown streets of the city were packed with people and all in one way or another were carousing. It was after saloon hours, but every bar opened for business, and did it. Grave and reverend seigneurs became splendidly drunk and all went merry as a large number of marriage bells. Toronto had known no such scene of revelry up to that time and has seen none such since. There was a different and a lighter feeling over the South African War than there was over the Great War in Europe thirteen or fourteen years later. I remember as a very small boy sitting at the upper window of a drug store in Toronto and seeing some very dusty and weary troops march up John Street, home from the North-West ruction of '85. The people were mildly interested. When the men came back from South Africa there was extraordinary rejoicing. They had gone a long way for their baptism of fire and blood and had acquitted themselves well. Some who had gone did not return, and memory of them did something, I think, to strengthen and swell the outburst of patriotic pride which welcomed the living when they came. After the World War there was a difference. That stupendous tragedy had bitten too deeply into the homes and hearts of the Canadian people to permit a welcome for the home-coming army that was not tempered by a profound and abiding grief. There were no Pretoria nights during the World War.

.   .   .   .   .   .

I still look back with shame to the occasion on which I scooped the scooper. A scoop, dear friends, is an item of news which the other paper does not get. It is highly prized by editors and a reporter with a good record of scoops to his credit may get a rise in salary if he lives long enough.

The Canadian Northern Railway built a line from Toronto in the general direction of James Bay (it never got there), and, having completed construction as far as Parry Sound, commenced operation by running a special train. I was on it and will never forget it. Where they got their rolling stock was a matter of sprightly if nervous speculation on the part of the guest-passengers. It used to be said that Mackenzie and Mann launched their railway enterprise on a shoe-string. If so, the string had been lost before this train was put together. The engine limped painfully, hot-boxes were numerous and, in general, the journey was replete with surprises, chief of which was our arrival at Parry Sound.

But about the scoop. One of the other newspapers had sent a young reporter who, apart from the fact of his having secreted a typewriter in the baggage car, was a very nice fellow indeed. During the latter part of the trip he repaired unostentatiously to his machine, wrote an account of the journey up to that point and, on the next occasion when the train broke down near a telegraph office, he filed his story, also in secret. By some strange mischance the product of his enterprise was not delivered to his newspaper but to mine. There it was scrutinized with suspicion but, as there was no name on it, the presumption was that I had been affected by the deleterious hospitality of Messrs. Mackenzie and Mann, and it was printed, thus demonstrating that the race is not always to the swift nor the bottle to the thirsty. I think my colleague and rival was disappointed. Undoubtedly he was surprised. But it was an accident and not my fault and he bore me no malice. Poor fellow; the last time I saw him was in the mud at Valcartier when, being in the ranks, he said good-bye to me with a facial contortion. He fought through the war unscathed until the taking of Vimy Ridge. I hope that in some way he can know that the sculptured glory which crowns that battlefield, perpetuating for ever the valour of that day, is there in his memory.

*   *   *   *   *

In 1901, the South African War being over, there came to Canada Their Royal Highnesses the Duke and Duchess of Cornwall and York, afterwards George V of beloved memory, and his Queen, who is now Queen-Mother. The late George Bennett, who then combined the duties of news-editor of the Toronto *Telegram* with high official duties in the Masonic Order, informed me that I was to go to Montreal to report the Royal visit and the behaviour of the populace. "You know Montreal well, of course?" he questioned. "Certainly," said I, having passed through the place as an infant in arms.

At the Windsor Hotel in Montreal I found myself rubbing shoulders with the entourage, including some famous British journalists, Melton Pryor of the *Illustrated London News*, E. F. Knight of the *Morning Post*, Maxwell of the *Standard*, Vincent of the *Times*, and so on, most of them internationally-known war correspondents. Their Royal Highnesses occupied Lord Strathcona's brownstone mansion on Dorchester Street West, and sentries marched up and down outside the gates. The Duke, as he appeared to me, was a somewhat reserved, very quiet, possibly a little shy, but a dignified and manly gentleman. He had been, as everybody knows, a sailor and was generally reputed to have retained a sailor's consideration for his grog. The Duchess was magnificent, a handsome, stately, and withal a very kindly and gracious princess. These two were destined to reign over England and the Empire during long years of progress and trial, to pass through the agony of the World War, to prove themselves the father and mother of the nation and to see the throne of Britain strengthened and its prestige enhanced while other monarchies were tumbling to the dust.

The Montreal visit was not the success that it might have been. The death of Victoria was still recent; the weather was bad, and William McKinley, President of the United States, was being assassinated in Buffalo. There was, however, plenty of excitement, a great procession, flags and bunting everywhere, nocturnal illuminations, a round of visits to universities, hospitals, etc., and a distribution of honours from the newly-enthroned Edward VII.

From Montreal we went to Ottawa, where the sun shone and where there were some interesting happenings, the most impressive being a distribution of medals to veterans of the South African War, Sergeant E. J. Holland of Ottawa receiving the Victoria Cross for saving the guns at Lillefontein. There followed the long succession of officers, privates, and nursing sisters and, at the last, a very tragic figure, Trooper John Mulloy, khaki-clad, standing bravely erect, but seeing nothing of the gorgeous spectacle around him, the hill of Parliament bathed in the golden sunshine, the blaze of colour, the silent throng, the future King bending to pin the medal on his breast, the far-off hills to which all there but he could lift their eyes. Mulloy had been blinded in the war. That and worse things happened many times in the great conflict which was to come later, but these tragedies were seen in a different perspective in 1901, and Mulloy, moreover, was fighting his terrible disability so gallantly that he had become a national hero, a national example and inspiration—and a parsimonious, mean-spirited Parliament haggled and disputed about a meagre pension for him, whereas nowadays a pension is rather difficult to avoid.

Things were done on the river. We went upstream, and were loaded onto rafts of square timber such as were common in the early days of lumbering on the Ottawa but are now, I believe, seldom if ever seen. On these huge cribs we ran the timber slides at the Chaudière, the newspaper raft going first, an arrangement apparently based upon the thought that if anything was to go wrong, the victims would be those members of the party who could most easily be spared. However, nothing did go wrong, and, the foot of the slides being reached, the adventurers climbed into canoes manned by Abitibi Indians and were paddled down to Rockcliffe, where from the balcony of the Ottawa Canoe Club they watched a war-canoe race and an exhibition of log-rolling, not the kind done in the neighbouring legislative halls, but the original, a sort of dance by rivermen on floating logs. It is, of course, an old art and it requires a great deal more practice and skill than is necessary in the log-rolling with which the public is more familiar.

The visiting newspaper correspondents were entertained in the press rooms of the House of Commons and a spirituous time was had. At, or about, the first stage of what may be called the mellow period, John Ewan of the Toronto *Globe* made a little speech. Ewan was one of the best editorial writers of his generation and a charming and lovable personality. He had been a war correspondent in South Africa and on the occasion of this bibulous reception he told of having been lost late one afternoon on the veld. He had

wandered about with no idea of his whereabouts
until, reaching the banks of a stream, he had come
upon an elderly gentleman, a nice old party, sitting
under a large green umbrella and placidly preparing
his evening meal.   The stranger had befriended
Ewan, had given him food and comfort and had set
him upon the right road.   "I never saw him again,"
said John, "until tonight.   He is sitting over
there," indicating the chubby form of Melton
Pryor.   There are moments when even Anglo-
Saxons do not stop at the cold and rather silly
formula of shaking hands; these two rushed at each
other, embraced and hugged each other, while the
rest of us, after the manner of Jamshyd, gloried and
drank deep.

The royal party went westward from Ottawa
and I went back to Toronto, thereafter giving
readers of the *Telegram* eye-witness descriptions of
the western journey from my desk in the office.
Later, the royal train being eastbound and nearing
North Bay, I was instructed to go north and board
it.   Finding that if I followed the directions given me
I would get to North Bay after the train had left
there, I waited at Huntsville in Muskoka and was
on the little station platform in the morning when
the train came in.   But they would not let me on.
The arbiter in these matters was Major F. S.
Maude, military secretary to the Governor-General,
Lord Minto.   This officer was from the British
Army and had become noted in Canada because of
his mental and physical inflexibility, mental because
he was a disciplinarian first and last, and physical
because his uniforms were made that way.   He did
not condescend to see me, but simply issued his

ultimatum of non-admittance. Fortunately there were newspaper men on the train, associates and friends of mine, who realized that this would not do at all. They went to Major Maude and made certain representations to him, the nature of which I did not know but was able to guess. He listened, was convinced and gave his lordly consent in the following terms: "Oh, let the fellow ride." I was a long, long time living that down. I am not quite sure that I have done it yet. But this same Major Maude was in a later time General of the British Army in Mesopotamia, one of the most brilliant leaders that the Great War produced. He died in the course of that terrible campaign.

．　　．　　．　　．　　．　　．

One of my experiences on the *Telegram* serves to illustrate the truth that a newspaper story may be the result of good luck rather than good management. In 1910, a hardy Scandinavian adventurer from Cleveland, a man by the name of Larsen, undertook to navigate the turbulent Niagara River between the Falls and Lewiston, passing through the world-famous rapids. I was sent over to see him do it, a staff photographer going along. Great crowds assembled in joyful anticipation of what was believed to be certain tragedy. For a variety of reasons the start was not made on scheduled time. The crowds went away and I with them. It was a summer day and the beer on the New York side was very cool and refreshing. Larsen—and for this I have never forgiven him—got into his specially constructed motor-boat, after the sight-seers had gone, and actually made the hazardous journey,

although the boat finally drifted to shore out of
control.

I was among the absent but, very fortunately
for me, my photographer, an Irishman, obedient to
some hunch or perhaps some Celtic inspiration, had
remained in the vicinity and succeeded in getting
the sole and only photograph taken that day as a
record of a very daring enterprise and a somewhat
dubious conquest of a natural element. I got my
facts from him and, with a liberal addition of
atmosphere, succeeded in deceiving the readers of
the *Telegram* in the belief that I had been hiding
somewhere in the boat. I don't think Barney
Gloster, good soul, ever gave me away.

Had this man Larsen been drowned, as he very
nearly was, and as had been considered mathematic-
ally certain, he would have been just one more
lunatic who had gambled with death and lost.
Instead, he became a hero in a small way. Success
does make a difference. When one Charles A.
Lindbergh began his flight across the Atlantic in
the *Spirit of St. Louis* the great American public
with one voice dubbed him the Flying Fool. When
he got to the other side he was the Lone Eagle,
and the same great American public took him to
their hearts. He is not there now, but that is
another story.

· · · · · ·

Excursions, such as the one I have described,
were agreeable interludes. They relieved the monotony, being brief escapes from the drudgery of police
reporting and the daily entertainment of the
Toronto public with more or less fanciful accounts

of police court proceedings. Not that the latter were without their moments. There, and in the civil courts, even the most indifferent listener learned something of the law, more perhaps of the lawyer, and a very great deal of the human species, moral turpitude and the profundities of human misery. Magistrate Denison, as everybody knows who knew him at all, was anything but a legal ritualist, certainly anything but a formalist. He held to the unusual belief that justice is more sacred than the law, and that belief he invariably put into practice. But his justice was tempered many, many times with mercy. His weakness for old soldiers was known to every thief, wife-beater and drunkard in the community and not one of them ever failed to exploit it and, in minor cases, to benefit from it. Many of them were bottle-scarred veterans, whose only fields of conflict were the floor of a bar-room or the adjacent roadway, and whose principal adversaries were the professional bouncers employed by the more thoughtful purveyors of alcoholic fluids.

I was glad enough to get away from an almost daily contact with unpleasant things and disagreeable people, from a routine which included practically every form of violence, its perpetrators and its victims, and with death in a nearly infinite variety. I have seen this strange and at the same time commonplace phenomenon under the most sharply contrasted conditions. I have seen Church and State uniting to honour their departed servants and have trodden softly amid the sombre splendour with which wealth in a last loyal gesture, albeit a gesture of bewilderment and futility, surrounds its dead; I have seen death in places of poverty and misery where living was nothing more than a slow process of dying, and have been in the presence of equal, if not greater, sorrow there. I have seen the broken bodies of men and women under the horribly revealing light of that most miserable of all places, the morgue, sometimes before and sometimes after the business-like post-mortem butchery of a police surgeon. I have seen the frightful corpses of people drowned, the horrible remains of people murdered, and some of these were little children—all part of the day's work, but to me, at least, never nice and, from the point of view of the most important of all theological precepts and promises, never anything but confusing. So, when one day John Ross—we never called him anything but that—informed me that I was to go to Ottawa and report the proceedings of Parliament, I was nothing loath. "You will be dealing," he barked, "with a different class of criminals."

4

The Nation's Eyes and Ears

WHEN QUEEN VICTORIA placed her pudgy but powerful finger on that part of the North American map where the capital of the new Dominion of Canada should be, the business of lumbering was flourishing up and down the Ottawa River and Bytown was one of the industry's strategic points. Much of the present wealth of the place had its origin in the forests of the Upper Ottawa Valley and the valleys of tributary streams, and at the opening of the century the fortunes of the lumber pioneers were in the possession of the original builders, or were passing into that of their heirs and assigns. Except for governmental expenditures, the wealth of Ottawa, now a great and growing city, springs from this source. The fact is not of much importance, perhaps, except as showing that there really was something in the neighbourhood before officialdom and the civil service arrived and took possession of it.

The late Dennis Murphy, who operated a transport fleet on the Ottawa River, and prospered greatly thereby, was able to remember the time when sheep grazed on Parliament Hill. They still do. In a still earlier day the Hill was a meeting-place for Indians and the Parliaments which meet there now conform to both these traditions.

I got to Ottawa on the evening of March 11, 1903. There was no Union Station in that comparatively dark age and Canadian Pacific trains drew into a station at Broad Street, whence, in the absence of taxi-cabs, the passengers proceeded to their hotels, or to one or other of the numerous parliamentary boarding-houses by street car. I did this and Senator "Wully" Gibson, then a power in the Liberal party, swayed from an adjoining strap. The Russell House where I was to live then and long after—there was no Chateau Laurier—was, I suppose, one of the most remarkable hostelries to be found anywhere in the world. It was a vast and ancient building with a great rotunda which was the meeting-place of politicians, job-hunters, contract-seekers, etc., from every part of Canada and of visitors from every corner of the world. It used to be said that the Dominion was governed more from the lobbies and rooms of the Russell House than from the ministerial offices or from the House of Commons. From my own experience I am inclined to think that this was measurably true, that what was decided upon in the Council Chamber and, where necessary, translated into law by

Parliament, had its beginning more often than not within the Russell's old grey walls. In its spacious lounge, its dining-room, and its somewhat dingy suites this venerable hostelry was an unofficial clearing-house for every kind of official business. It has gone now, but its history, if any single individual could have known and written it, would have been the history of Canada over a very long period, and some of it would have been unprintable. After establishing myself at this very favourable spot on the night of my arrival, I drifted into the offices of the *Ottawa Citizen*, into which was coming just at that moment the first news of the Gamey scandal in the Ontario legislature. I have something to say about R. R. Gamey. The Liberals, it will be recalled, being in rather desperate need of support, were accused of having tried to buy the "Man from Manitoulin," and the ensuing rumpus marked the beginning of the end of a long Liberal régime in the province. The Conservative slogan then was: "Where did the money come from?" The question was never answered, at least publicly, but it was answered to me by a member of the Liberal organization of that day, who for some reason or other admitted me to his friendship and confidence. I dislike disappointing a possibly interested reader, but what he told me was not intended for any ear but my own, and so far as I am concerned it remains a secret.

Robert Roswell Gamey, whatever his other faults and virtues may have been, was one of the most accomplished spell-binders I ever heard. In the winter of 1903-1904, the Ross Government was fighting with its back to an extremely fragile wall and there was a critical by-election in the North Renfrew riding. E. A. Dunlop, later to be a Conservative Minister, was the Opposition candidate and the contest was waged in sub-zero weather. There was to be a meeting at Chalk River, one of the earth's coldest places, and Gamey was billed to speak there. A party of us set out from the town of Pembroke for this meeting. We were packed onto some sort of open bob-sleigh and had a long way to go. It was bitterly cold and notwithstanding fur robes and fur overcoats the journey was one of acute discomfort. There is a peculiarly malignant winter wind which blows across the Petawawa Plain and any one who likes it can have it. Furthermore, the majority of us, indeed all but one of us, had no oil in our lamps. The story of the Foolish Virgins was paralleled up to the point at which the one prudent member of the party produced a bottle of rye whiskey and—departing from scriptural precedent—passed it around. I am sure that he saved our lives. Arrived at Chalk River, we proceeded to a little schoolhouse, or something of the kind, consisting of a single room heated by a big stove and as hot as the rest of the world was cold. This room was filled to overflowing with as intensely and unanimously hostile an audience as could have been got together in any one place, and Gamey was the object of their fury. They manifested a decided inclination, if not a determination, to tear him limb from limb. This was at the beginning of the meeting. Gamey mounted the little platform—and made no speech. He did not, that is to say, utter anything approaching the usual campaign oration; instead, he talked as man to man in a conversational tone, never lifting his voice, arguing but never attacking, and in some way giving the impression that he was taking these Chalk River men into some inner chamber of his heart. The sequel was amazing. The crowd, which had been murderously antagonistic at the outset, got up as one man and, pushing and squeezing to the front of the hall, shook him by the hand and slapped him on the back. It was a complete conversion, and it was not a case of hypnotism. I don't know how we got back to Pembroke, but we did. Dunlop, by the way, was elected.

. . . . . .

The Press Gallery, when I went there, was divided on party lines almost, if not wholly, as distinctly as was the House of Commons, and the government news, official announcements and what not was exclusive to the Liberal correspondents. This had its advantages and also its disadvantages because no newspaper correspondent in the confidence of the Government had anything like the latitude which was open to his competitors. He could not indulge in intelligent anticipation or, indeed, in any kind of anticipation, but was bound and gagged by the responsibilities of a partisan journalistic connection. On the whole the opposition correspondent had much the better time. By putting two and two together, he could upon occasion beat the Liberal side of the Gallery at its own game, and if he was only nearly right it was good enough. But a newspaper man in the Ottawa Press Gallery, if he was worth his salt, was usually much nearer right than wrong, and if he was not worth his salt he did not last long in that select company. The pace was too fast and the requirements of the newspapers of that day too exacting. I don't think anybody ever extracted any news out of Laurier. He was kind and courteous to all; but the celebrated sunny smile was all they got for their questions. Fielding was worse. My own belief is that he would not have admitted being Minister of Finance or even of going by the name of Fielding without satisfying himself that his inquisitor was not seeking to entrap him into the disclosure of a Cabinet secret. Moreover, no employee of his department, big or little, with the possible exception of that excellent man, J. C. Courtney, who was Deputy Minister long ago, ever dared call his soul his own except as a solo performance, a soliloquy or something of that kind. The other ministers and their staffs, while careful enough, were not averse to occasional conversation on official subjects, and among the private members, the senior men, who moved about the edge of the government circle, there were friendly souls who were not above opening their hearts in secret to a Conservative correspondent whom they could trust. Moreover, there was one class of news of an official or semi-official sort that the Opposition correspondent could get and his Liberal competitor could not. There were times, and doubtless there will be again, when a cabinet minister, finding himself in a tight corner, has given his confidence to an Opposition newspaper correspondent, has sought his help and has received it. For instance, the head of an administrative department is anxious to have his ministerial colleagues agree to some proposal which he thinks good, but they hold back, usually as an expression of political cowardice. What does the first-mentioned minister do then, unburden himself to a journalist of his party? Certainly not. He goes to a friendly opponent with whom he holds sweet communion, and the next day half a dozen newspapers in different parts of the country are telling their readers upon semi-official authority of a new government enterprise which is likely to receive early consideration. Public opinion begins to operate, if the policy involved is acceptable, and the hand of the reluctant ministerial majority is forced. If the kite fails to remain in the air, no one suffers. The minister disclaims all responsibility and all knowledge respecting the leak, and the correspondent, for the life of him, cannot remember where he got his information. Then there are incidents of official announcements finding their way into the newspapers too soon. When the Duke of Connaught was Governor-General there was an official earthquake over one of these mishaps. A woman somewhere in the Province of Quebec had been sentenced to death for murder and, as the execution date approached, the fate of this unfortunate creature had become a matter of acute public concern. Quebec did not like the idea of hanging a woman, but it began to look as if the sentence would be carried out. Late one afternoon I was going down Elgin Street and fell into step with a member of the Government who had just left a cabinet meeting. "We commuted the sentence of that woman," he said casually. "Did you?" I replied. "That was nice of you,"—or something of that sort, and I left him hurriedly, the telegraph office being near by. The next day there was a smell of brimstone in and about the East Block. The commutation had not received the Governor's signature and His Royal Highness was furiously enraged. The Government had been on the carpet and a most unpleasant time had been had by all. There was talk of an inquisition but, of course, none was held. All that happened to me was that one of the confidential secretaries came to me and said, "I suppose if you were asked who gave you that information, you wouldn't tell." I assured him that his supposition was accurate in every respect.

At another time a very enterprising correspondent announced two knighthoods in advance of the formal communication, and the Governor-General was so incensed that he refused to make the recommendations, and two very distinguished citizens had to remain plain "mister" until there was another honour list and no premature disclosures. Their wives were very angry.

.   .   .   .   .   .

I am not sure that the Ottawa Press Gallery now is as exclusive an organization as it was thirty to thirty-five years ago, but when I went there it was a very close corporation, extremely jealous of its rights, most if not all of which were assumed. It followed a convenient British precedent in that it had no written constitution, so that its seniors were in a position to apply such rules and regulations as they saw fit when dealing with newcomers and upstarts. The Gallery was, and is, a self-governing body, claiming and exercising as complete an autonomy as even Mr. Mackenzie King could ask in behalf of the Dominion, or Mr. Hepburn in behalf of Ontario. Theoretically there is some responsibility to the Speaker of the House of Commons, though its character and extent were never precisely defined, since no Speaker ever knew anything about it and no man in the Gallery ever brought the matter to an issue. Like the House of Commons, the Press Gallery when I knew it first had its traditions. These were handed down by word of mouth and were illustrated more or less by yellowing photographs upon the walls depicting richly bearded gentlemen of bygone journalistic ages. Newcomers were assured that these had been giants in their day and that no beginner need ever hope to attain a sagacity, a literary distinction or an influence equal to theirs. This was depressing to those who believed it. Also the Gallery had its politics. Each year it elected a president, a vice-president, a secretary, and an executive committee, and these officers collectively exercised the high justice, the middle, and the low. They exacted unimpeachable credentials from every new arrival. The most determined attempt to dispute their jurisdiction was made by an individual who came down from the Yukon, who had credentials of sorts but whose interests and activities lay outside the newspaper field. He claimed to be of royal descent, and looked it, and was in no way abashed by the fact that his shield, if there had been one, would have borne the bar sinister. He had friends in the Government and in due course they sent him to an official position a long way off where he embarrassed them extremely by flaming forth in a resplendent uniform to which he was not in the least degree entitled.

Sometimes the Gallery itself was torn by its own political storms. Being young, I was induced to participate in these internal ructions, which may account for the fact that I passed in due time through all the offices. For a long time the Gallery was divided into two bitterly hostile camps, so that men who should have been friends hardly spoke to one another, but the breach was healed in time and the conflict forgotten. There was no one, I am sure, who wished to remember it or who looked back upon it with anything but regret.

The Gallery always had and has still, I am glad to think, a kindly welcome for its former members. They used to appear on budget days and other important occasions but, in 1903, the Old Guard of the photographs had all gone, with, I think, one notable exception—Edward Farrar, one of the ablest and most resourceful and versatile journalists that this country has ever had. He was a short, stocky, ruddy and bearded man with a twinkling eye and a mind stored with state history that he had helped to make. It was said that in one of the Macdonald elections he fought valiantly on both sides simultaneously, but I fear this story belongs to the political Apocrypha. I knew him in his later years and came willingly enough under his spell. Other men who had served in the Gallery had passed to editorial positions in various parts of Canada. Many others had drifted into the civil service as secretaries to Ministers or in other capacities and a number of my own contemporaries sought the security and tranquility of that haven. Others went to the omniscience of editorial chairs, some went into business and some became states-

men.   The Honourable Fernand Rinfret, Secretary
of State and former Mayor of Montreal, was for a
time a Gallery correspondent.   Colonel the Honourable J. D. Taylor of New Westminster was, if I am
not mistaken, a page in the House of Commons
before he became a newspaperman, a member of the
House, the owner of a newspaper, a soldier and
finally a senator.   Many others who have won
distinction in their profession or in other walks of
life are, or were, old members of the Press Gallery
and no one of them still living ever forgets it.

Members of the present Press Gallery will forgive
me an expression of personal opinion.   It is that the
annual Press Gallery dinners nowadays are less
attractive than they were in former years, at least
as recalled in old men's memories.   The contrast is
between quantity and quality.   In these days the
Gallery has at its head table the Governor-General,
His Majesty's representative, but it has also, sitting
as it were below the salt, almost every Thomas,
Richard and Henry who can pay for a ticket or cadge
an invitation.   This, to my mind, is not as it should
be.   It is possible that, in the almost pre-historic
period to which my thoughts go back, we were
governed to some extent by a limited accommodation, but, whatever the reason, we picked and chose
very carefully in the selection of our guests, and the
result was that an invitation to an annual Gallery
dinner was something which the ordinary run-of-
mine member of Parliament prized above rubies.
We held these dinners in the subterranean dining-
room of the House of Commons, a comfortably
furnished oblong chamber which, for some reason
or other, we called the Ark.   There were half-a-

dozen fixtures at these gatherings, the Prime
Minister, the Leader of the Opposition, the Sergeant-
at-Arms, two railway publicity men—George Ham,
the immortal, and Harry Charlton, representing
the Canadian Pacific and Grand Trunk Railways
respectively—and John Knight, who at that time
filled a somewhat similar role for the Canadian
Bankers Association and was one of the most fertile
story-tellers, one of the most agreeable companions
known to a fortunate generation. Sir Wilfrid
Laurier never missed these functions, never ceased
to enjoy them. He would rise in his turn and in
the graceful phrases for which he was famed would
assure his hosts that there were no men like them,
and he never failed to say, "I, too, was once a
newspaper man." The revelry was always
restrained, whatever may be said of the informal
proceedings subsequent to the dinner itself. Anecdotes were told but they were always more or less
decorous, the narrators being conscious of the fact
that Sir Wilfrid was a bit shy of the more extreme
smoking-car brand. He was frightened half to
death on one occasion when George Ham began the
Story of the Hired Man, and was on pins and
needles until the great George, who had deliberately
prolonged the agony, brought his narrative to a
perfectly respectable close.

When Colonel H. R. Smith was Sergeant-at-
Arms he was, of course, always a guest, and always
he recited, with moving emotion, John Hay's full-
bodied epic of the Mississippi, "Jim Bludso." He
was never called upon until the champagne had
gone around at least half-a-dozen times. It was
considered necessary that he should be on the verge

of tears. Never was the Gallery weary of hearing Jim Bludso's heroic assurance, "I'll hold her nozzle agin' the bank till the last galoot's ashore," and never was the Colonel's lugubrious rendition of the line received with other than prolonged expressions of tumultuous joy. The good old Colonel finished his last recital many years ago.

I am told that there was a philosopher once who comforted himself with the reflection that even God could not take from him the dinners he had eaten. Surely no beneficent deity would wish to take from any one even the memory of those old Gallery banquets, of an atmosphere that can never be recaptured of a company for ever disbanded. We think kindly of our old friends now, and we thought kindly of them then, but we dissembled our love. We subjected our guests to literary abuse and their only consolation was that we were no more sparing to ourselves. On February 29, 1908, we received them with Thomson's "Welcome, kindred glooms, congenial horrors, hail." Of ourselves we said, "But where we are is Hell," a line from Marlowe, and we went to Rabelais for "God send fools more wit and us more money." Two years later the toast to our guests was accompanied by Jerome's excellent advice, "It is always the best policy to speak the truth, unless, of course, you are an exceptionally good liar"; and Swinburne provided us with the question, "What ailed thee, then, to be born?" Some one must have relented a little, because I find also a question from Smollett, obviously genuine, which runs, "I'll be damn'd if the dog ha'n't given me some stuff to make me love him." We were rather good to ourselves that year, calling Arnold to witness that we were "Slaves of the lamp, servants of light," but there was some little conflict between Pope's, "And conscious virtue still its own reward," and the practical Boswell's blunt statement that, "No man but a blockhead ever wrote except for money."

In one later year, I have forgotten which, the Gallery prepared and distributed among its dinner guests a little red book patterned after the *Parliamentary Guide*. It contained the most candid biographies ever assembled in one volume. The *Parliamentary Guide*, for the benefit of those who have not seen it, is a small book published annually and semi-officially. It contains records of federal and provincial elections, a list of members of the royal family, something about the Governor-General and biographical sketches of all privy councillors, senators, and members of the federal and provincial legislatures. As these sketches are supplied for the most part by the persons concerned, they suggest a modest reticence as to all unfavourable characteristics and all discreditable deeds. The Press Gallery production was a departure from this tradition. Not only did it hold the mirror up to nature, but it held it in such close proximity that nature herself showed symptoms of embarrassment. As this had been the intention, the authors of the publication may be said to have achieved their aim. There were guests about that board who were reminded of matters that for years they had been endeavouring to forget, errors that for perhaps half a lifetime they had been trying to live down. But it was all good-naturedly done, delicately phrased, and every victim with one exception took it in good part. The exception was a man without humour, born, I fear, with that fatal handicap, a man almost incapable of laughter, one upon whose face I never saw a smile. The book went through only one very limited edition, and I doubt if a copy can be had now for love or money.

Songs, I am glad to say, are still sung at the Gallery dinners, as they were years and years ago, songs made up for the occasion, most of them semi-humorous, others blatantly slanderous. In the days when Mr. Fielding, still professedly a low tariff devotee, was administering the Department of Finance as a competent if not an enthusiastic protectionist, he was invited to the festive table, where he was treated to a variation of "Put on your old grey bonnet."—"Put on your free trade bonnet with the red ribbon on it," etc., and the minister smiled sardonically. That was a mild example compared, for instance, with the treatment of the Honourable William Pugsley, who was Minister of Public Works during a very interesting and, as the Conservatives insisted, a very expensive period. Pugsley was popularly known as Slippery Bill, and at one of the Press Gallery dinners there was heard the pleasing air of "Has any one here seen Kelly?" But they were not talking about Kelly, or singing about him. It was Pugsley, and as the choir got into its stride it bellowed, "For he's Slippery Bill and he's slippery still, but he never slips when he's at the till," and so on. I am not able to remember whether the Honourable William was a guest on this occasion, but in all likelihood he was. No one would have enjoyed the vocal tribute more than he.

The Parliamentary Press Gallery is, as I have

said elsewhere, the newspaperman's university. When he has taken his degree, there is no place in journalism for which he is not qualified. There are, of course, exceptions to this as there are to every other rule, because characteristics vary, and vary widely, in any company of men. There have been brilliant writers at Ottawa who were never more than that. There were others with no such literary pretensions who developed marked executive capacity. There were, as there must always be, the specialists, and the Press Gallery has had these with a frequency proportionate to its numbers. It has had its Caesar and its Rienzi, its Rabelais and its Milton, its Galahad and its Casanova. It has had many Falstaffs and it has had its lean and hungry men. But all in all, it has been and is a company of able, conscientious and incorruptible men, loyal to the public whom they serve and to the high tradition of the institution whose honour is in their hands. And if long contact with officialdom and politics tends to breed in them a wary cynicism, they are saved from complete surrender to it by that sense of humour which is said to be divine.

· · · · · ·

The old Parliament Building, the central block which housed the Senate and House of Commons, was in my poor but honest judgment superior in some important respects to its successor. This present structure follows the general lines of its predecessor in exterior only, and whereas the old tower was beautiful, the new one is long and skinny, symbolizing perhaps a nation which has the unfortunate habit of sticking its neck out. True, some very lovely music comes from it; it is the singing tower; also the Peace Tower, but the original was musical in another and a better sense. From it came the harmony of beauty and of dignity. It was restful to the eye and soothing to the soul. It was old and mellow and within its shadow had lived and moved the men who gave this country its greatest laws and the greatest measure of prosperity it has ever enjoyed. The interior of the present building is a maze of Gothic exuberance. Only the library remains of the earlier edifice, an architectural wonder, but unfortunately invisible from any frontal point.

Also the old buildings had their history, and it will be a long, long time before the newer block has any history that will be fit for a possibly high-minded posterity. Everything in and about the place that I knew spoke eloquently of a mighty past. The entrance stones were worn down by the feet of legislators, statesmen, and leaders who had lived their lives and died and whose names have become imperishable. In the green chamber, the desks and chairs were the same desks and chairs that Sir John Macdonald, Alexander Mackenzie, Edward Blake, the eloquent D'Arcy McGee, Cartier, Chapleau, Dorion, Langevin and all the others great and small had used since the first days of the Dominion. Out of that Chamber, on an April night in 1868, having uttered a magnificent plea for understanding and union, D'Arcy McGee had walked to his death at the hands of an assassin. The Chamber and the corridors, the rooms and offices throughout the Commons' wing, still seemed to me to hold the shadows of these men.

I am not familiar with the cellars of the present building, but the basements in my time were well worth visiting. The dining-rooms were there, one on the Commons' side and another for the Honourable gentlemen of the Senate, very quiet, cosy and peaceful places, where men lingered over appetizing food. And there were little rooms about. Nobody, so far as I am aware, ever knew their purpose, but many professed to know the interesting uses to which occasionally they were put. And there were bars in the vicinity, one for the stimulation of Commoners and one where the elder statesmen assuaged a thirst which, considered collectively, would have shamed a camel. The port on the Senate side was somewhat celebrated, but the Commons' bar could produce in an emergency a decoction of rum which was very comforting to the wounded heart. And the heart was very often wounded and required treatment. It was not considered proper to invite a friend or colleague down to the Senate bar to have a drink. There was a prescribed ritual which was rigidly observed. "Let us," the hospitable one would say, "go down and see the cornerstone." And the cornerstone was there, having been well and truly laid by the Prince of Wales who became Edward the Seventh. From the cornerstone the further progress to the bar was automatic, instinctive, inevitable. It was possible also to travel from the Senate bar to the Commons' bar and vice versa by slithering through a hole in the region of the furnaces. Sometimes it was prudent to pass that way.

Some years later the Laurier government erected an extension to the Commons' wing, which was an excellent thing for the gentlemen of the Press. Up to that time the press room had been some five sizes too small for the comfortable accommodation of the men who were telling the public from day to day some but not all of what went on in the neighbouring precincts. It was a square room with a nice big fireplace and alive with the legends of Louis Kribs, Tim Healey, Edward Farrar, John Willison, and other mastercraftsmen, who in one way and another had moved on. One veteran journalist died in that room. Another was found asleep there by the charwoman on a morning after a preceding night, and when they attempted to disturb him their delicate sensibilities were outraged by a richly embellished resentment. They sent for the housekeeper, a bewhiskered factotum whose practice it was in season and out to wear an embroidered skull cap of very ancient vintage. This unhappy mortal endeavoured to do what the charladies had failed to do. The journalist urged him to vacate the premises and referred to him, inaccurately as it afterwards appeared, as "a baldheaded, old ——." Deeply mortified, the housekeeper repaired in haste to the Sergeant-at-Arms, that beloved old warrior, gone away these many years, Colonel Harry Smith. Into what I fear was an unsympathetic ear the wrathful one poured his complaint, winding up with a repetition of the epithet, which the sleeper awakened had employed. "And," said he, "Colonel, you know I am not baldheaded."

However, when the above-mentioned extension was designed, and eventually built, journalistic enterprise turned it to good purpose, securing for itself a long room across the front of the building.

This was achieved by the simple but effective method of "squatting." It was virgin territory; the newspapermen simply moved in and took possession. At the same time, and out of the goodness of their hearts, they left two or three of the smaller apartments near by for the use of Sir Wilfrid Laurier, the Secretary of State, and the chief Whip of the Liberal party, who was then Billy Calvert of Strathroy, or it might have been Jim Sutherland, later the Honourable James Sutherland, a member of the Government. Concurrently the Commons' bar moved from the ridiculous to the sublime. From its old home in the cellar it went up to the top floor, and the poor wretch who operated the elevator in that new wing had reason to wish that he had never been born. That upper room was nearly fatal to me, as will hereinafter be shown.

Before leaving this subject of structural enlargements and extensions, it may not be inappropriate to mention the little matter of the Laurier Tower. This regrettable business took place when the Honourable Charles S. Hyman, rest him, was Minister of Public Works. The Government conceived it to be its duty to enlarge the West Block by building to the north and rounding off the addition with a tower. The West Block housed a number of administrative departments, including Trade and Commerce, Railways and Canals, State, Inland Revenue, and possibly one or two more. Over it rose the magnificent Mackenzie Tower, then and now the finest on Parliament Hill. The new little tower was nearing completion when, on one sunny summer day at or about the hour of noon, and without any notice whatever, it collapsed and fell into a dismal ruin of stone and timber and dust, and the outside world was immediately and faithfully served with the news that the Laurier Tower had fallen down. Then the real trouble began. The association of the great leader's name with the shapeless heap of debris was considered ominous by superstitious people, while equally superstitious Conservatives were cheered and elated. But it transpired that the Tower had never been formally christened. Nobody knew, that is to say, very few people knew, how, when or by whom and why the name had been attached. When on several following days Conservative members rose in the House and twitted the Government on the downfall of the Laurier Tower, furious Liberals demanded to know, "Who named it?" The Honourable Jacques Bureau of Three Rivers, then Solicitor-General and afterwards a senator, was particularly inquisitive on this point. Nobody had the answer. Now, however, as Sir Philip Gibbs would say, it can be told.

The tower having come thundering down to the good earth, it occurred to a couple of Tory newspaper correspondents that somewhere at some previous time, both unknown, somebody had suggested the naming of the new tower in honour of the Prime Minister, who would thus be immortalized in masonry even as his predecessor, Mackenzie, had been. If any such suggestion had ever really been made, the author of it, especially if it be presumed that he was a loyal Liberal, could not have had foreknowledge of the weakness of the mortar. Nevertheless, to the corrupt and partisan minds of these two degenerate journalists, it seemed a good and proper thing that those who have towers named after them should take a little of the bitter with the sweet, whereupon, and at their nefarious hands, the recumbent tower underwent a post-humous baptism. The ceremony was simple. All that was necessary was to inform the Conservative newspapers of the country that the Laurier Tower had fallen down. Hence it was that although the tower had not stuck, the name did.

* * * * * *

There must be many active Canadians now who never heard of what used to be called the Dundonald Incident, but a little more than thirty years ago it was a matter of hot discussion in Parliament, in the country, and in the editorial columns of the English newspapers. It had been the custom to import British army officers to head the Canadian militia and permanent force and, in 1904, the Earl of Dundonald was established at Ottawa as G.O.C. Douglas Mackinnon Baillie Hamilton Cochrane, Baron Cochrane and twelfth Earl of Dundonald, a representative Scottish peer with a castle in Wales with an unpronounceable name, was a distinguished soldier and came of a line of soldiers and sailors, scientists, engineers and inventors. He was a Life Guardsman, had fought in the Nile Expedition in 1884-1885 and had gone across the desert to the relief of Khartoum. He had ridden furiously over the same desert with despatches announcing the seizure of Gakdul Wells and again with news of the death of General Gordon and the fall of Khartoum. He had been a cavalry commander in South Africa, fighting along the Tugela and at Colenso, and had gone at the head of his brigade to the relief of Ladysmith, where Sir George White with twelve thousand troops had been bottled up for four months. Physically handsome, there was still about him the aura of heroism by reason of his magnificent service in South Africa. He took his position in this country, seriously studied the organization and requirements of the militia and in due course drafted a number of proposed reforms. Everybody spoke well of him, including the Minister of Militia, Sir Frederick Borden, and others, who later on were to plunge their daggers into him. Unhappily, Dundonald's understanding of democracy as exemplified on this continent was imperfect. He had to learn that the Canadian militia owed its appointments and promotions in a very large measure to political influence and the exercise of political preferment. When he made the discovery he was displeased, and probably disgusted. Nevertheless, he determined to make the best of a bad job and to proceed with his project of creating a citizen army of one hundred thousand men, trained and ready for service, and a second line of equal strength. Then the little thing happened, the little spark that always causes the explosion.

There were some regimental appointments to be made in the Eastern Townships of Quebec, the political preserve of the Honourable Sydney Fisher. Also there was some urgency about it. The G.O.C. made out his list for the approval of the Council and, in the temporary absence of the Minister of Militia, it passed through the hands and under the protruding eyes of the Minister of Agriculture. Political lines were sharply drawn in the Townships and the Honourable Sydney was wont to cherish his partisan hatreds and to exercise them when this could be done with safety. In Lord Dundonald's list he believed he saw the influence of his most formidable party foe in the Eastern Townships, and he promptly erased one of the names. Shortly afterwards Lord Dundonald attended a military banquet in Montreal, supposedly a private affair, and spoke his mind with soldierly directness on the undesirability of mixing political and military matters. His strictures were promptly made public and the fire was full of fat. Both Houses of Parliament took the matter up, as did the Canadian and British press, and, to make matters worse, Sir Wilfrid Laurier, speaking in the House of Commons, referred to Dundonald as a foreigner. He corrected himself immediately, but the fire blazed still more merrily. There was very general sympathy with the G.O.C., but even those who felt with him experienced some difficulty in justifying his action. Fisher, a gentleman farmer and very, very much a civilian, had the astonishing effrontery to assert that in deleting the name of the prospective officer he had done so upon the ground of military unfitness. This was the only note of comedy in what was, in all other respects, a very serious controversy and Fisher himself made no attempt to keep the joke going. His later defence was a political tirade against his opponents in the Townships, their oxen and their asses and everything that was theirs. To the everlasting shame of all concerned, himself excepted, Lord Dundonald was dismissed and returned to England. I saw him shortly before his departure and I am certain that he was more nauseated than hurt. He had acted according to his convictions, had cared little or nothing about the consequences to himself, but had been genuinely and earnestly concerned about the Canadian Militia and its efficiency. There is no doubt that he went away consoled with the belief, unfortunately unfounded, that his sacrifice had not been in vain. He had not been in Canada much more than a couple of years and had not learned that the Canadian politician, with but few exceptions—and most of these die young—puts politics first and other considerations nowhere. It is scarcely surprising that, ten years later, with an unprecedented crisis to be faced, the Canadian Militia was still, to a very large extent, a political machine.

. . . . . .

Of the great Liberal chieftain much has been written and some of it has been correct and just. Laurier was not a person but a personality. His two principal assets were his distinguished appearance and his exceptional oratorical ability. These things inspired in his followers a love and loyalty that no other leader in this country, not excepting Macdonald, has ever possessed. People of his own race thought and spoke and wrote of him not as a man but as a god. Though not an aristocrat born, he was one by nature and adaptation, a gentleman by instinct. His party placed him upon a pedestal and for the greater part of his premiership he was rendered immune from direct attack. I had little to do with him and he did not like the things I wrote about him. "I have read," he would say, "some of his work and for my part I do not want to read any more." But when business took me to him I was received, as were all others, kindly and graciously. He was easily the foremost leader of his own time, but beyond the qualities which I have mentioned his equipment was inferior to that of his principal opponent, Sir Robert Borden. Neither of these men had what the other possessed. Borden was vastly inferior to Laurier as a speaker. It took him a long time to forget that he was not arguing in a court of law. On innumerable occasions he would stand in his place in the front rank of the Opposition and hitch an imaginary gown over his shoulders. There was no magnetism about him and Laurier had it in abundance.

Conservatives who recalled the endearing frailties of Sir John Macdonald grew restive under the consistent propriety of Mr. Borden's public and private life. They were heard at times to express the wish that their leader would some day embark upon a Bacchanalian burst, would roll down Sparks Street and heave a brick through a plate-glass window. It was a vain hope. But Borden was by no means a man without emotions or the ability to express them. In the House of Commons he was savage when roused. Elsewhere he could, when put to it, speak in a language which, though it might pass in a present day drawing-room, could not have done so then. Furthermore, he could be, and was among his intimates, the most cheery and interesting of companions. Though his appetites were controlled, he was not a teetotaller and could enjoy the society of men whose indulgences were under no such restraint. He liked his cigar and at bridge he was not only an agreeable opponent but, a much more severe test, an agreeable partner. He liked his golf and had a fund of stories that were good, if rather cleaner than most. I saw him on the western prairie on a winter day throwing snowballs at a railway engine. But he never had the personal charm which Laurier could always exert, and his relations with his followers in the House were in no sense comparable with the bond of personal devotion by which Laurier held his own supporters. Nevertheless, Borden was in a number of important respects the abler man of the two. He was a better lawyer. Upon non-political matters his judgment was more dependable. Where Laurier was superficial Borden was profound, and in the routine business of manufacturing laws the Conservative Leader's superiority was never open to question. I enjoyed Sir Robert Borden's friendship for thirty years, was with him in success and in adversity, and while in some respects and in some circumstances he failed to fulfil the accepted conditions of leadership, particularly during his long period in Opposition, I will say that in character he had few major defects, and he was the intellectual equal of any of his contemporaries. He lacked at times the power of decision and he was never adept at handling men. At least twice, prior to 1911, groups of Conservatives in the House conspired against him, and at one of these times, I know, the question of his continuance in the leadership hung in very delicate balance. Borden was discouraged and disgusted and was very nearly going back to the practice of law. Fortunately for himself and for this country, he was persuaded to remain.

Upon another occasion a call was sent to Richard

McBride, Premier of British Columbia, to come to
Ottawa, the purpose being to turn the leadership
over to him.   Dick McBride was a picturesque
person as well as a successful politician.   He
possessed an elegant figure, was smooth of face and
smooth in his ways, and easily dominated the
political picture in his own province.   He affected
the Macdonald-Laurier hirsute style, with a mop
of silver hair at the back of his head.   Laurier, you
will remember, entered one of his later campaigns
with the battle-cry, "Follow my white plume."
For some obscure reason Laurier feared McBride,
possibly because of the general similarity in their
facades, but more probably because of the British
Columbian's extraordinary hold upon his own
province—later to be lost—and the potential danger
which lay in his then apparently growing strength.
Whether or not McBride came to Ottawa with full
knowledge of what the conspirators had in mind I
am unable to say, but having arrived there he
cannot have remained in ignorance of what was in
the wind.   The method pursued was interesting
and somewhat original.   Borden was to be eaten
out of his position and talked out of it.   An elabor-
ate banquet was prepared by the Judases, though
not in an upper room, and there was a full turn-out
of the party.   That Borden should be asked to
speak first in the post-prandial proceedings was
unavoidable.   What he did was unpredictable.   He
got to his feet and delivered one of the finest orations
of his career, an aggressive, fighting, forceful speech
which lifted his hearers to their toes, and when,
later on, McBride was called upon, his address was
an anti-climax.   The Parsifal from the Pacific, who

had been brought east to wrest the jewel of office from the Liberal Templars who guarded it, went home again. That plot had failed.

Some years later, such are politics and politicians, one if not more of the quondam intriguers accepted ministerial preferment from him and, as members of the Government, behaved after their kind. Reid became a Minister, and thereafter stuck to his leader like a sinister shadow, passing from a minor to a major portfolio, and some of his work is with us yet and will be with us for a long time to come. W. B. Northrup, after a period of probation, if not of contrition, was made Clerk of the House of Commons. Sir Robert Borden's capacity for forgiveness was the marvel of many.

The House elected in 1896 was at least as interesting as any of its successors. Close to the Conservative leader lolled the huge form of John Haggart, who at the time of Confederation was Mayor of Perth and who had served in the Macdonald, Abbott, Thompson, Bowell and Tupper Administrations, and had been one of the famous "nest of traitors," the sextet of ministers who left the Bowell Cabinet on the fourth of January, 1896, and went back on the fifteenth. He had been in the House since 1872 as member for South Lanark, and at this time was not much more or better than an indolent relic of an age gone by. Hugh Guthrie was there, later to leave the Liberal party and to become a Conservative minister and in due course a railway commissioner. Duncan Fraser, a great bulk of a man, sat for Guysborough. He had been a member of the Legislative Council of Nova Scotia and was to be Lieutenant-Governor of that

Province. Also he had been Grand Master of the Nova Scotian Free Masons. I walked home with him one night from a lodge meeting in Ottawa and the architectural contrast was embarrassing to us both. A very fine man was this Duncan Fraser.

George W. Fowler, from King's County, New Brunswick, exemplified a different type; the same Fowler who originated the parliamentary classic, "Wine, Women and Graft." Down from Provencher, Manitoba, had come the Honourable Alphonse Alfred Clement Lariviere, a former provincial secretary of Manitoba, exceedingly fat and equally futile. Colchester, N.S., had sent Seymour Eugene Gourley, noted for his startling sartorial eccentricities. White duck trousers and a black frock coat would never have surprised his colleagues, even to an accompaniment of tan boots and a sombrero, though, I think, he never went quite that far. He would begin a speech in the region of the back benches and conclude it at the desk of the Hansard reporter, upon which desk he would pound furiously, to the acute discomfort and alarm of the scribe. Once he brought his little boy to Ottawa. He took him to dinner at the Russell House. "Pop," piped the little boy, in the gleeful hearing of a dining-room full of people, "what is an Independent?" "A damn scoundrel, my son," was the reply. Not a bad definition, though somewhat too comprehensive. For instance, Frank Oliver, who had carried his little newspaper press across the prairie in an ox-cart and had patiently published the Edmonton *Bulletin* under formidable frontier difficulties, was still an Independent with a seat far back among the Liberals. True, he

became progressively less Independent and at the
end of the process was appointed Minister of the
Interior, but at no time during the period of his
Independence had he merited the Gourley description. He had the gift of tongues, one of which was
suitable for polite conversation and the other was
not. His parliamentary speeches were delivered
with extraordinary intensity and suggested an
outboard motor addicted to backfiring. One of the
pastimes of the more light-hearted legislators in
those days was to send a note to this speaker or to
that in the hope of interrupting his train of thought.
An innocent little page boy took one of these
missives to the Honourable Frank in the midst of
one of his staccato performances. He knew the
game. His speech went on unbroken, except for
the inclusion of one word: "Getthehelloutofhere."

Oliver was accustomed to the old-fashioned
newspaper office, where the odour of the ink was
all-pervading. In later years I took him through
the *Gazette* composing-room in Montreal, where he
walked upon a soundproof floor amid lines of steel
type cases, everything about him spotless. He had
only one comment: "It doesn't smell right."

The Honourable William Paterson was Minister
of Customs and one of his achievements had been
the defeat, in 1872, of Sir Francis Hincks, Minister
of Finance in the first Macdonald Cabinet. Paterson
was a good old soul with one of those voices which
are said to afflict the dead with insomnia. There
is a story told of him, which I suspect had been told
of others also. At an evening sitting he was
replying to an Opposition critic, who at the close of
the afternoon deliberations had gone to Montreal.

"I am sorry," he bellowed, "that the honourable member is not now within the sound of my voice." "Don't worry," interjected a helpful Conservative, "He'll hear you!"

Another story, no doubt equally apocryphal, was told of Thomas Mackie, a giant of a man, an Upper Ottawa lumberman who had beaten no less a person than the Honourable Peter White in North Renfrew. At the time of the Manitoba school controversy, Mackie was reported to have said, in a moment of expansive party loyalty, "What is this Remedial Bill? I'll pay it myself."

Others of that day were Colonel David Tisdale, whose grandfather had fought at Queenston Heights and Lundy's Lane, who himself enlisted at the time of the Trent business, was a Fenian Raid veteran and had been Minister of Militia in the Tupper Administration; Sir Charles Hibbert Tupper, who had served in his father's Cabinet; Honourable Jim Sutherland, Minister of Public Works and former chief Liberal Whip; Charles S. Hyman of London, who later succeeded Sutherland and, when the Laurier Tower collapsed, fervently thanked God that the Department was not building it; Colonel Sam Hughes, who is to be heard of later; still others who became judges or senators, and many more who had their day and ceased to be. One man occupied a political compartment of his own, John Charlton of North Norfolk, a strong advocate of reciprocity with the United States, a lecturer and author, one of the founders of the Lord's Day Alliance and author of the Charlton Act for the protection of women and girls. It used to be said that John

Charlton had too much ability to be a member of any government. My own belief is that his principles were too strong.

. . . . . .

The Canadian Senate of 1903 was in many respects a remarkable body, particularly in regard to the historical background of its senior members. There still survived in this branch of Parliament men who had been active contributors to the success of the Confederation movement. They were not extraordinary men in most respects and few, if any of them, had been able to envisage in 1867 the tremendous progress of the Dominion which they had helped to create. Some of them had supported the Confederation project, not as an ideal, but because of their conviction that the disunited provinces, if left to themselves, would meet with disaster. Not many of them were left, but there remained such living links with the pre-Confederation past as Sir Richard Scott, Sir Mackenzie Bowell, the Honourable Andrew MacDonald, the Honourable Wm. Miller and Dr. Charles Eugene Boucher de Boucherville.

Sir Mackenzie Bowell had sat in one House or the other ever since the first Dominion parliament assembled in Ottawa. For a full quarter of a century he had represented the Ontario constituency of North Hastings in the House of Commons. He had been Minister of Customs under Macdonald, Minister of Militia under Abbott and Minister of Trade and Commerce under Thompson. On the death of Sir John Thompson, Sir Frank Smith, as Senior Privy Councillor, recommended Bowell to

Lord Aberdeen for the office of Prime Minister.
Bowell is said already to have intimated his determination, or at any rate his willingness, to sponsor
legislation in the interests of the Roman Catholic
minority in Manitoba. It was never suggested by
any one that he was actuated by anything but a sense
of justice. He was an honest man and, moreover,
an Orangeman of the highest rank. His was not a
happy ministry. In his short term of less than a
year and a half as Prime Minister, his government
was threatened by the sudden resignation of a group
of his colleagues—the "nest of traitors"—and, a
few months before the fateful general election of
1896, Sir Charles Tupper replaced him. Bowell
was blamed for many years, and perhaps rightly,
for the disaster which overtook the Conservative
government and party in 1896, but he never blamed
himself and the closing years of his long political
career were spent quietly and serenely in the com-
parative tranquility of the Upper House, where he
was generally liked and universally respected.
The Federal Department of Trade and Commerce
was organized by Sir Mackenzie Bowell and the
Colonial Conference of 1894 was originated by him,
and he presided over it.

Senator Andrew Archibald MacDonald of
Charlottetown had not only moved about the pre-
Confederation stage but was one of the only two of
the Fathers of Confederation living in 1903. Sir
Charles Tupper was the other, and Tupper at this
time was in England. Senator MacDonald, therefore, was the one man alive in Canada who had
attended the Charlottetown Conference of October,
1864, and the Quebec Conference held two months

later. He was in his seventy-third year when I knew him, white-haired and white-bearded, but mentally he was marvellously alert and could recall and discuss the events of fifty years before as clearly as if they had happened yesterday. Born on Prince Edward Island, he had been a store-keeper and ship-builder and then, for fifty-seven years, he had been in politics, serving in the Island government, harassed by the economic problems of the little province, and he would tell how real was the danger of secession and annexation prior to the Union. He was looking back to the days when trading was done in kind, and the only money circulated was minted in the United States, whither went most of the Island's products. Out of the economic distress of that time had grown the movement for a Maritime union, and out of that movement the Confederation project. Senator MacDonald took what he believed were the only notes of the Charlottetown Conference taking during the deliberations, what the newspaperman would call the only running report. When I talked to him these notes were still in his possession or in that of his family in Charlottetown. What ultimately became of them I never knew, but if they are not among the treasures of the Dominion Archives they ought to be. This grand old gentleman spoke to me of the Charlottetown meeting, of the arrival of the "Canadians"—Macdonald, Brown, Cartier, Galt and others—of the decision to meet again in Quebec, and of what was accomplished there. If Sir John Macdonald was tepid in his support of the Confederation Movement, and some have said that he was, the Island senator saw no evidence of it. "Sir John," he said, "neither rested himself nor allowed the others to rest until a decision had been reached." At Quebec the delegates were not even allowed a luncheon adjournment. Would the course of history have been altered if the issue had not been determined on empty stomachs?

William Miller came from Nova Scotia and had been a Conservative there in the days when the redoubtable Joseph Howe was waging his great fight for responsible government. He was one of the original senators appointed by royal proclamation in 1867 and, by 1903, he had outlived all those who had entered with him. At seventy-six he still remembered Nova Scotia's flirtation with secession. He had been a member of the colonial legislature from 1863 up to the time of the Union. He had favoured the Union in principle, had striven to bring about the Confederation agreement but, in common with other Nova Scotians, had vigorously opposed the terms proposed at the Quebec Conference. It was he who suggested the Conference in London of 1866, whereat the terms were revised, and Nova Scotia swung into line.

At a later day there was to enter the Senate another Nova Scotian of colonial vintage—the Honourable William Ross, a Liberal and one of Senator Miller's ancient adversaries. It happened on a day that these two worthies met on the long walk leading down from the Parliament Buildings to Wellington Street, and that the old political fires flared up. The debate waxed warm until one of these patriarchs denounced the other as a "toothless viper," whereupon he was promptly challenged to a foot race down the Hill. It was one of the great griefs of Ottawa that this challenge was never accepted. It cannot be accepted now.

Dr. Charles Eugene Boucher de Boucherville, if not a Father of Confederation, nevertheless had some standing as a maker of Canada. In 1903, he was one of the oldest living legislators, a hale old man of seventy-six, one of the three ex-Premiers then sitting in the Senate, a tall and stately gentleman, so vigorous and strong that time, it seemed, had passed him by. He traced his ancestry back through a long line of seigneurs of New France to one Lieutenant-General Pierre Boucher, Sieur de Grosbois, who was governor at Three Rivers in 1653. Senator De Boucherville had sat in the Canadian Assembly as member for Chambly from 1861 until Confederation, when he entered the Legislative Council and became a member of the Chauveau provincial ministry. From 1874-1878 he was Premier of Quebec, but in the latter year had run foul of the Honourable Luc Letellier de St. Juste, Lieutenant-Governor, who thought that his authority was being slighted. St. Juste threw the De Boucherville Government out bodily. The evicted Premier went to the Senate but, in 1891, on the fall of the Mercier government, he was back in Quebec and in his former office. He remained there two years, at the end of which time he resigned of his own accord. Senator de Boucherville had the unique distinction of holding seats simultaneously in the upper houses of both Ottawa and Quebec, practically in two Senates. He has gone now, with his fine figure, his bushy head, his roman nose, and his rich store of the folklore of his native province.

Of the other senators who were present in that year, I think only two are living now—the Honourable Raoul Dandurand, Government leader in the Red Chamber, and the Honourable J. P. B. Casgrain, who seems somehow or other to have found the secret of eternal youth.

5

The Railway Binge

It WAS to this Parliament that the Grand Trunk Railway came in 1903 with its application for the Grand Trunk Pacific charter. It was the beginning of a tragedy of which I was an eye-witness, but not, I am thankful to say, *particeps criminis*. The Grand Trunk, with the astute Charles M. Hays at its head (drowned years later in the sinking of the *Titanic*) had developed a perfectly natural desire to share in the growing traffic of the North-West. The Canadian Pacific had built the country, but neither the Grand Trunk nor the Canadian Parliament considered that this service vested any kind of proprietary right in the C.P.R. or, indeed, any right at all. The whole history of railway expansion from 1903 onward has been a record of indifference to the people who really colonized the West; and I am not referring so much to the paid officials of the C.P.R. in Montreal and elsewhere as to the great number of investors, big and little, who put their money into the enterprise, trusting to a national good faith which turned out to be a very broken reed.

The Grand Trunk idea was to construct the Grand Trunk Pacific across the prairies with a connection down to North Bay, and the plan was sound enough.   To the everlasting misfortune of the Dominion, the Government and Parliament took upon themselves to enlarge this plan and to insist upon structural specifications which involved so heavy an overhead that the project was doomed almost from its inception.   Sir Charles Rivers-Wilson, head of the English Board whose absent treatment had always been a drag upon the Grand Trunk, came to Canada to get the Western charter, and he and Mr. Hays appeared before the Railway Committee of the House of Commons.   Sir Charles very nearly saved the situation for the Canadian taxpayer by assuming an attitude of feudal arrogance toward the Committee.   Briefly, he was telling the colonials what they had to do and the colonials were for throwing him out neck and crop, bag and baggage.   Hays, however, was a different type, an American, suave and persuasive.   He knew all about handling politicians and if he had forgotten anything the astute and hospitable Mr. William Wainwright, whose car stood upon a neighbouring siding, filled the gap.   Hays took the platform after Rivers-Wilson had demonstrated his native ability to spill all the beans that were spillable. The troubled waters were liberally oiled; the wrath of the Committee subsided; the situation was saved or rather, as we know now, it was lost. The politicians had seen this opportunity. Quebec and the Maritime Provinces, particularly New Brunswick, demanded a share in the spoils, and so insistent were they that an arrangement was made between the Government and the Grand Trunk whereby the former should build a line across the northern wilderness of Ontario and Quebec and reaching down into New Brunswick, crossing the St. Lawrence by way of the Quebec Bridge, which had been projected by a private company with strong Liberal leanings. Nor was this all. The Government and Parliament insisted that the new line in the West should be built to the standard of the old Grand Trunk, a stipulation which was unnecessary, uneconomic and in the end disastrous. The National Trans-Continental, which the Government undertook to build, was to be leased to and operated by the Grand Trunk. It was to be a grain road, since there was not an ounce of traffic available in the territory through which it would run, and it was to supply a golden stream of traffic for ports on the Atlantic. The House of Commons fought all that summer and most of the next over the Grand Trunk Pacific charter, or rather an amended charter, but Laurier persisted in regarding this new Trans-Continental as his crowning achievement. He so regarded it notwithstanding the fact that his Minister of Railways, Andrew G. Blair, would have nothing to do with it, that he left the Government on account of it and from the seat of a private member condemned the whole programme in one of the most vigorous, carefully reasoned and at the same time one of the bitterest speeches ever heard from the floor of Parliament. Laurier had said, "We cannot wait because time does not wait." Blair said: "We cannot wait because Senator Cox cannot wait."

It is not often that an Opposition is endowed with the gift of prophecy, but if any one is sufficiently interested in this old story to go through the Debates of 1903 and 1904 he will find there a forecast of practically everything that has happened to the country by reason of this railway programme, and of what happened to the programme itself. The Grand Trunk Pacific was built at immense cost, while the National Trans-Continental was a nightmare for all concerned, with the exception of some of the contractors. More than one Parliamentary investigation was held into charges arising from the conditions under which this line was constructed. The cost was so great that the Grand Trunk lost no time in backing out of its bargain and the Government was left with a finished and useless road and the necessity of providing a service over it. The Grand Trunk Pacific was well located, magnificent hotels were built at Winnipeg and Edmonton, and for some years things went well enough, but the company had been saddled with too heavy a financial burden and the time came when another government—the Borden Ministry—was informed by the parent company that, "We are at the end of our tether."

The things that were said by Laurier, Fielding *et al* in support of the Grand Trunk Pacific-National Trans-Continental would sound in these days as diverting as a Gilbertian libretto were it not for the critical difficulties that have come upon the country by reason largely of those nonsensical utterances. Incredible as it may seem, Laurier actually did assure Parliament that construction of the road was a national and commercial necessity and a corollary to our status as a nation. Absurd as it may appear, he did say that if the opportunity were passed "the voyage of our national life, bright as it is today, will be bound in shallows." And this scintillating gem: "We cannot wait because time does not wait; we cannot wait because, in these days of wonderful development, time lost is doubly lost; we cannot wait, because at this moment there is a transformation going on in the conditions of our national life which it would be folly to ignore and a crime to overlook. . . ." It is equally true that he said the building of all these needless miles of railway was a duty "immediate and imperative," a duty "not of tomorrow, but of this day, of this hour and of this minute. Heaven grant that it be not already too late; heaven grant that whilst we tarry in dispute, the trade of Canada is not deviated to other channels, and that an ever-vigilant competitor does not take to himself the trade that properly belongs to those who acknowledge Canada as their native or their adopted land." And he added: "Upon this question we feel that our position is absolutely safe and secure; we feel that it corresponds to the beating of every Canadian heart." It still does, and very painfully.

One of the main arguments advanced by the Liberal leader was that the United States Government might make up its mind to cancel the bonding privilege under which Canadian trade went to and from American ports, as it still does. He quoted Andrew Carnegie as suggesting that the United States had in this bonding privilege a club with which it could prevent extension of preferential trade between Canada and Great Britain, and he dug up some old speeches by President Cleveland and President Harrison. He was very much in earnest about this, notwithstanding the fact that withdrawal of the privilege would have deprived United States Atlantic ports of a very substantial trade which only this bonding privilege permitted them to enjoy. But it was in discussing the financial aspects of the new railway project that Laurier excelled himself, and his Finance Minister after him. He still thought that the National Trans-Continental would be operated by the Grand Trunk on a three per cent. rental basis, as per contract, and he solemnly assured the House that, with the exception of a few years of interest, "we shall have this portion of the railway built by the Government from Moncton to Winnipeg without the cost of one dollar to the Canadian people." The Government would advance the money and pay interest upon it but would receive interest at the same rate from the company, "so that whatever we give with one hand we shall receive back with the other."

Then as to the Grand Trunk Pacific. This was not to be operated by the Government because that would involve the construction or acquisition of steamships, the sending of agents to Asia and elsewhere, the business of hotel building and hotel keeping—all the various related enterprises in which succeeding governments have been engaged.

Furthermore, Sir Wilfrid was greatly mistaken if the terms of the contract with the Grand Trunk Pacific would not "astonish friend or foe with their superior excellence." He insisted that the Government's financial liability would be limited to the payment of interest on the company's bonds during the first seven years and that, mark this, "the sum total of the money to be paid by the Government for the construction of that line of railway from Moncton to the Pacific Ocean will be in the neighbourhood of $12,000,000 or $13,000,000, and not a cent more. Now, sir, what is thirteen millions in the year 1903? The surplus of this year will pay for the construction of this road." It all sounds very funny now or would but for the hundreds of millions that are actually saddled upon the Dominion as the price of this exuberant eloquence.

It is fair to say that Sir Wilfrid was not a businessman, that he was never any good at figures, other than those of speech. His deficiencies in this regard might be cited now as ground for absolution but for the embarrassing fact that he was backed up by the one man in the government who should have known what he was doing, the Minister of Finance. Mr. Fielding was a very able routine minister, but upon the two occasions when he attempted major political and financial enterprises he came to grief. He was hopelessly wrong in regard to this Grand Trunk Pacific-National Trans-Continental project, and his reciprocity bargain with the United States seven years later sent his party out of office. On August 12, 1903, he told the House of Commons not only that the Laurier figure of thirteen million dollars was substantially correct as expressing the total cost of the railway programme to the country, but he came near arguing that there need be no cost at all. What he said was this: The capital account of the Eastern Division will amount to $54,609,676 and upon this the Dominion will pay an annual interest charge of $1,638,290 for seven years. All the Government need do would be to hand over the sum of $8,853,504 to an insurance or trust company or any other companies dealing in annuities, for investment at three per cent. half yearly. The $8,853,504 could be taken out of the federal surplus for that year, used in the way suggested and all would be well. The minister did not say that he proposed following this remarkable course; nevertheless, he submitted the proposition as actuarily sound. Then as to the Grand Trunk Pacific section, again by actuarial calculation —and Mr. Fielding asserted that he had consulted an actuary—the Government was committed to pay only seven years' interest upon the cost of the mountain section up to a limit of $14,400,000. Again all that would be necessary would be to take $2,334,575.90 out of the current federal surplus and submit it to the same process as already described, and presto, the seven years' interest charge on the mountain section would be covered completely. It sounded too good to be true, and it was. Yet the public swallowed it. "We firmly believe," said Mr. Fielding in concluding his speech, "we will be able to give to the Dominion of Canada one of the greatest achievements in its history." Well, they did, probably the greatest of all achievements in the realm of when not to do it and how not.

And these men were the leaders in what was considered a great Government. That they were honest in the presentation of their railway policy and in their estimates of its costs is, I think, beyond question; that they were incompetent to deal with an enterprise of such magnitude is beyond argument unless there is to be found someone with sufficient hardihood to wrangle with history and with the national debt and with the tax-gatherer.

The Opposition leader, Mr. Borden, condemned the product in all its essentials, estimated the public cost at $100,000,000—which was very far below the ultimate loss—and offered as an alternative the extension of the Intercolonial Railway to the Georgian Bay, whether through the acquisition of the Canada-Atlantic (the Booth line) or otherwise, the nationalization of the Canadian Pacific from North Bay to Fort William for joint use under joint operation or that of an independent authority, and the granting of some assistance to the Grand Trunk Pacific for the construction of a line north of the Canadian Northern in the West as far as Edmonton or some adjacent point. Mr. Borden enlarged upon the advantages of this substitute scheme, which in fact had much to commend it, but both Parliament and people had surrendered to a delusion of grandeur and for that pathological lapse we are now paying.

Opposition members analyzed the Government project from the standpoint of structural difficulties, from the point of view of traffic and traffic destinations, and all who went into the question of cost disputed the Government's estimates as hopelessly wide of the mark. They wasted their time, and their energies and their breath. No later than the next session Sir Wilfrid was back in the House of Commons with an amendment to his wondrous contract, an amendment which gave the Grand Trunk Pacific promoters far more liberal terms, terms so extravagantly generous that Sir Robert Borden was moved to propose that the country should own the road since it was obliged to pay for it.

It is one of the great mysteries of public life and the administration of public affairs that a party in office invariably forgets what it learned in opposition. The Borden Government took over the Grand Trunk Pacific. It committed the country heavily in its efforts to save the Canadian Northern, though it took forty millions of the company's common stock, and when Mackenzie and Mann also found themselves at the end of their tether—or shoe-string—their railway became Government property. There is a story which explains why the Canadian Northern, which had a well-fortified western system, was extended eastward through Ontario. Railway men know it, or some of them do, and some politicians must know it still better, if any of those responsible for an iniquitous example of political jobbery are still alive. The Borden Government, in deciding that these railways should not be permitted to go into bankruptcy and that they should become publicly owned, acted upon broad principles of public policy, but the credit of the Dominion, which was the object of this expensive solicitude, is more in jeopardy now than it was then. The old Grand Trunk was subsequently taken over, upon terms which ever since have been the subject of protest, by shareholders, which occasioned long litigation and which, rightly or wrongly, soured the

British money market against Canadian issues for twenty years.

The Laurier Government had poured public money and public guarantees into the Grand Trunk Pacific and into the Canadian Northern, besides building the National Trans-Continental monstrosity upon the stupid assumption that it would function as a wheat road feeding Canadian Atlantic ports. It has never been a wheat road and, if it had been, there would have been no west-bound traffic and the grain trains from the West would have been obliged to go back empty. Whether or not the old Grand Trunk could have retained control of the Grand Trunk Pacific under any conditions is problematical; but what was intended as a western feeder could never have been anything else than a heavy drain upon the parent company for the reason that the physical standard established by the politicians was unnecessarily high and the Grand Trunk Pacific Company was compelled to operate under a crushing capital obligation. Had the old Grand Trunk been permitted to carry out its own project in its own way the results might have been reasonably satisfactory. And had the Canadian Northern in the West been linked with the Grand Trunk in the East—there were some abortive negotiations to this end—a sound condition would have obtained. Even had the Canadian Northern, at a later period, come to an arrangement with the Canadian Pacific instead of extending its lines east of Port Arthur—and were not there some negotiations to this end also?—the final outrage in this unlovely railway chapter would have been averted.

It is all spilt milk now and there is not much use in crying over it, but the record has some value as showing how all this muddle came about, how the people of Canada were betrayed by their elected representatives thirty-five years ago, and how the curse of public ownership was brought into the Canadian railway field. And to go back to 1903 again for a moment, so that we may all be rendered a little more uncomfortable. The Dominion Government's total revenue on Consolidated Fund Account, in 1903, was very slightly more than $66,000,000, and there was a surplus of well over $14,000,000. The total revenue from taxation in that memorable year was under $50,000,000, considerably less than half what is now being collected under the Income Tax alone. Moreover, the total liabilities of the Dominion stood at the ridiculously low figure of $361,344,098. It is scarcely necessary to compare these modest sums with the appalling totals of the present day. The difference is not, of course, all attributable to the period of railway lunacy, but if there had been no such period we would all now be sleeping much more peacefully in our beds.

·   ·   ·   ·   ·   ·

In 1906, Finance Minister Fielding, with a perhaps subconscious but none the less discriminatory sense of fitness, altered the federal fiscal year. Up to then it had commenced on Dominion Day. Since then it has commenced on All-Fools' Day. As a matter of fact, it was not long after this timely alteration that the financial trouble began and the public debt started on its upward flight towards the stratosphere. Of course the cost of the war made matters infinitely worse, but if there had been no railway orgy the war debt would have been easily manageable.

. . . . . .

Those hard-working early sessions were prolonged almost to the limit of human endurance, but they had their moments. There was, for example, the June day in 1903 when the Press Gallery played the House of Commons at cricket on the green lawn of Parliament Hill. Within easy reach of the crease there had been erected a large and commodious marquee, liberally stocked with stimulants. It was not one of the happiest days of my life, because I had spent the night before, meaning the whole of the night before, in conference with that grand old veteran, Robert M. McLeod, somewhere back of the office in the Russell House. The subjects discussed had been Scotland and the potable products of the Highlands. It was not a good way to prepare for a cricket match, even in competition with a House of Commons eleven. Neither McLeod nor I participated actively in the day's proceedings, but we were stalwart witnesses. The Commons' team was captained by E. A. Lancaster and had among its members Mr. R. L. Borden of Halifax, Seymour Gourlay of Colchester, J. S. Copp, E. D. Smith, the Jam King of South Wentworth, both the latter two in after years passed into the Senate. Still another player was Walter Scott of the old territorial riding of West Assiniboia, who was to become first Premier of the Province of Saskatchewan. Of the Gallery contingent, five are still living; Arthur B. Hannay, described in the official programme as Dealer, Fred Cook, who had been Mayor of Ottawa and was correspondent for the London *Times*. He was long stop. J. D. McKenna of Saint John, N.B., appeared in the list as half-full-back and H. F. Gadsby as caddy. The fifth survivor is Arthur Beauchesne. He was inside-home, and, oddly enough, still is, a somewhat capricious fortune having carried him into the office of Clerk of the House of Commons and left him there in a silken robe, with a large rosette at the back of his neck. The others are all gone, including such then well-known journalists as Tremenhere Passingham—first base; William McKenzie—left wing; W. H. Dixon—full-back; and and J. A. Garvin—pitcher. It was a fine, bright day and, if the running between the wickets was indifferent, that between the crease and the tent distinctly good. So far as the cricket match was concerned, the Commons eleven won, but the Gallery beat them badly in the marquee.

. . . . . .

We have gone a long way from these spacious days when at the opening of every Parliament a generous tax-paying public presented each member and each senator with a large, handsome and expensive leather trunk, the same delicate courtesy being extended to members of the Press Gallery, probably as a judicious precaution against untimely and ill-advised publicity, the tax-payer being for the most part unaware of his own liberality. The beneficiaries were always too modest to mention it. And at the commencement of every session the same deserving servants of the people each received a small wooden trunk stuffed to the lid with every known variety of choice stationery—paper, pads, pencils, pen-knives, paper-cutters and so forth and so on. Also, more often than not, there was something extra by way of good measure, a fitted leather case or a valise or, as on one occasion, a particularly attractive lady's work-basket. All of which largesse was received in a becoming spirit of gratitude but was fiercely opposed and resented by non-recipients on moral grounds. But, since time changes and men change with it, there came upon the scene at last the Honourable Charles Murphy, occupying the office of Secretary of State and also that of Minister of Parliamentary Loot. He refused to act in the latter capacity, and none of the receivers of stolen property dared make an issue of it. Not that the tax-payer got anything out of it. There isn't a man or woman in that category who would not now very willingly give up the income tax, or the sales tax or the excise tax, or this or that other impost, and let the members have their trunks again.

6

Laurier and the Talents

Laurier in 1903 was at
the height of his popularity and power. I had not
seen him for seven years. He had spoken in
Toronto in the general election campaign in 1896,
addressing a great meeting in Massey Hall and an
overflow in Shaftesbury Hall. He had been given a
great reception. Sir Charles Tupper had also gone
there, and I can still see the old "Warhorse of
Cumberland" standing on the platform of Massey
Hall, waving a copy of the *Evening Star* and bellow-
ing his opinion that it was a dirty, filthy rag, though
one of these adjectives would have been sufficient.
The *Star*, needless to say, had been vigorous in its
condemnation of the Remedial Bill, which was the
main campaign issue. Tupper made his speech
because he could out-shout even a Massey Hall

audience, but Emmerson Coatsworth, sometime Mayor of Toronto, could get no hearing at all. He was a supporter of the Remedial Bill and lost his seat in East Toronto to John Ross Robertson, running as an Independent on the slogan, "Hands off Manitoba."

By 1903, the Manitoba school question was becoming a forgotten issue and Thomas Greenway, who had been Premier of Manitoba when the separate school storm broke, was occupying a seat in the House of Commons, a very quiet, perfectly useless and inconspicuous old gentleman. Not so his Attorney-General, Clifford Sifton. That astute politician had blossomed into one of the ablest and most influential members of the Laurier Cabinet. He was more than Minister of the Interior; the Interior, which was the whole North-West, was in the hollow of his hand and it was a very steady hand, very sure and, on occasion, very heavy. Sifton poured settlers into the country—that was his contribution to Canada. He broke with Laurier, in 1905, over the original school clauses of the Saskatchewan-Alberta Autonomy Bills, and most of the Western Liberals went with him. When they all came back, they did so on Sifton's terms. Then, in 1911, the same Sifton was vigorously opposing the Laurier reciprocity agreement with the United States and was employing his organizing genius in behalf of the Conservative party—as strange a bedfellow as politics have ever made. Clifford Sifton left his mark upon Canadian history. He died in 1929, a man of substance, and a knight. He had stalked across the political stage, self-contained, self-assured, and strong in an intellectual superiority which warranted the contempt which he had for his opponents and, it must be believed, for some of his colleagues also. If he was ruthless, he was also efficient, and if he achieved a great personal success it can at least be said that he made a great and lasting contribution to the country's development.

The first Laurier Ministry was called the Cabinet of all the Talents. It was not that. It was the usual geographical, religious and racial mixture of ability and mediocrity. There will always be such cabinets in Canada until their composition can be rendered independent of sectional and doctrinal considerations. The theory of comprehensive representation as applied in the making and remaking of governments has deprived and will continue to deprive the Dominion of the possible maximum of efficiency in its governing bodies. I stood close to the operation of this theory over a period of many years and the results have seldom been good, except of course to the third or fourth-rate politician, who could not have hoped to enter any government under his own steam.

I think it can be said that this Ministry was above the average, and most of the original members were still functioning in 1903. The formidable Sir Richard Cartwright, crippled with rheumatism, and savagely resentful of sympathy, was still Minister of Trade and Commerce, a master of precise English, and one of the most polished speakers in a House whose oratorical standard was very high. But he was a bitter and cynical old Tartar. On one occasion the Opposition, smugly virtuous, as Oppositions always are, was holding up its hands in monastic horror at the iniquity of one of Sir

Richard's henchmen in South Oxford. Cartwright got to his feet with difficulty, suffering, I am sure, excruciating pain and inwardly blaspheming. His glasses glared, his monstrous moustache bristled, and he said, "I am not addressing a girls' school in this matter." Poor old Sir Richard, a great figure in his day and it was a long day, but who remembers him now?

David Mills, who had succeeded Sir Oliver Mowat as Minister of Justice—the "Little Ol" who had reigned for so long in Ontario—had been replaced in turn by the Honourable Charles Fitzpatrick, promoted from the post of Solicitor-General, destined to be Chief Justice of Canada and Lieutenant-Governor of Quebec, a gentleman of outstanding ability and of great personal charm. He had no special reason to befriend a newcomer in the Press Gallery, much less a representative of the Toronto *Telegram*, but when he had help to give it was never withheld.

Then there was Sir Frederick Borden, cousin or something of the Leader of the Opposition, tall, debonair, fruity of voice, a joyous old boy and something of a scamp, who could play the fiddle at a supper party if it was the right kind of supper party, and who had other qualities which for the sake of delicacy are usually called human. He was Minister of Militia and contributed to the gaiety of nations. I liked him.

William Stevens Fielding was, of course, Finance Minister. He had been Premier of Nova Scotia and, taking him all round, I am inclined to think that the public life of Canada never had a better man in it. He was fussy and inclined to be sus-

picious, but he was an able and progressive administrator, thoroughly sound in his general policy, a
man of unblemished integrity and a very, very loyal
Liberal. He was Laurier's right-hand man, but it
was taken for granted that he could never be more
than that because the Province of Quebec disliked
him. He had the limitations which sometimes
cling to men from the Maritimes, but he also had,
and in large measure, the great qualities of mind
and the sturdiness of character which have placed
so many of those men in the highest positions which
the fields of politics, education, finance and commerce have to offer in every part of the Dominion.

Fielding was the father of the British preference,
a Free Trader by profession and a Protectionist in
practice. The contradiction is not uncommon and
is seldom harmful. But Fielding had a vulnerable
heel. He wanted reciprocity with the United
States, although his leader, after one rebuff, had
proclaimed that there would be "no more pil-
grimages to Washington." With the requisite
academic qualifications he might have shone as a
schoolmaster. As Finance Minister he presented—
notwithstanding the respect in which he was held—
the not uncommon combination of personal rectitude
and political dishonesty. He was one of the
provincial premiers called by Laurier to his first
cabinet in 1896. As head of the government of
Nova Scotia, he had attained considerable prestige
and he went to Ottawa armed with it.

Perhaps he should not have been given the portfolio of Finance, because its successful administration involved the surrender or subjugation of his
political principles. His inclination had always been

toward a low tariff if not toward out-and-out free trade. As a Laurier minister, however, he was quick to conclude that continuation in office must be conditional upon adherence to the Conservative policy of tariff protection. It is not on record that he experienced any difficulty in adjusting his conscience to this fundamental change. It is a fact of record that he practised protection throughout his federal ministerial career. The Conservatives charged him with stealing their clothes and the accusation was all the more loaded with bitterness by reason of the knowledge that the theft had been committed by a free trader. Fielding, however, weighed against the displeasure and discomfiture of his political opponents the good will of the industries of the country, and he went on his way complacently.

It is fair to say of him that he did not enrich himself, indeed it became necessary in his later years to raise a fund in his behalf, but his official career was marked by opportunism and cynicism in an unusual degree. He should have left office in 1905 when the Laurier Autonomy Bills outraged his convictions, but he remained. He was a good administrator in the routine sense, though rigid and dictatorial, feared as much as respected by his subordinates, but he was one of those men to whom office was an end rather than a means and if a still, small voice was heard at times by him, he silenced it ruthlessly. It was Fielding who negotiated the Agreement of 1910-1911, which I may talk about a little later on.

Over in the Senate was the patriarchal Richard Scott, hale and vigorous at seventy-eight. He had been Commissioner of Crown Lands in Ontario under the Blake and Mowat Administrations, had served in the Mackenzie Government in the 1870's, had gone out with Mackenzie and come in again with Laurier. But as a member of the Senate from 1874 he had escaped the worst consequences of ministerial defeat. This political veteran was the author of two very important statutes, the Separate School Law of Ontario and the Canada Temperance Act, better known as the Scott Act. Much could be written upon either of these laws. A great deal has been said about them. Scott was knighted in 1909, having passed from the status of an individual to that of an institution.

Sir William Mulock, still alive at this writing and unbelievably old and hearty, is sole surviving member of the original Laurier Cabinet and, with the exception of Sir Charles Fitzpatrick, the only one left of the Cabinet of 1903. He was Postmaster-General, a big, bluff man, not, I am afraid, slow to anger—his occasional tantrums were terrific—but genial enough on the whole, a good debater and an exceedingly competent administrator. He it was who fathered penny postage and it was to him that the young Mackenzie King told his story of sweated labour in Toronto, with the result that the Department of Labour was established. Sir William would rise in the House, push away his chair, and present his case forcefully and, as a rule, convincingly. He would then sit down to an accompaniment of tumultuous Liberal applause. But on one memorable occasion, after a particularly striking peroration, he forgot about having moved his chair aside. He got so near the floor that only his head and voluminous beard remained visible.

Sir William passed from the storms of politics to the placid precincts of Osgoode Hall and rounded off a great career as Chief Justice of his native province. Now in retirement, he is a kindly, mellowed and benign old gentleman, the grand old man of Canada and universally revered.

Sidney Fisher was Minister of Agriculture and representative of the Eastern Townships; a total abstainer, a prohibitionist, an inveterate talker and in general a most insufferable person. He would lecture the House for hours on the manners and customs of insect pests, the domestic intimacies of pure-bred swine, and the most effective if the most primitive method of fertilizing agricultural acres. I may be exaggerating, but that is the impression that has remained with me through the years. He was a good enough minister, a pioneer in approved methods of marketing, including refrigeration of perishable goods in transit and the provision of cold storage warehouses in various parts of Canada. He helped the dairy industry, and in various ways contrived to promote the welfare of agriculture. But he was one of the most unpopular little men on Parliament Hill. His speeches were interminable and frequent and their only recommendation was that they appeared to occasion in him a distress almost as acute as that experienced by his hearers. It was a favourite practice of the Opposition to prod the Honourable Sydney as a means of wasting time and thereby deferring some other business for which the Conservatives were unprepared. Once when Mr. Fisher sat down, after one of his long and mutually painful orations, the Honourable John Haggart leaned across to his leader, Mr. Borden, and, in a quarter-deck whisper, roared, "Shall I ask the little beggar a question and get him going for another four hours?" It should be said, perhaps, that the descriptive term used here is not precisely the one which Mr. Haggart employed. This garrulous little busybody it was who sent Lord Dundonald out of Canada.

.   .   .   .   .   .

Any man who spends a few years in the Parliamentary Press Gallery hears and sees astonishing and amusing things. I have in mind an after-dinner debate on the subject of organized labour or something related to it. That fine old Tory gentleman, W. R. Brock of Toronto, merchant-prince and parliamentarian, had just expressed what would be called in these days reactionary sentiments, and there arose to reply a prominent Liberal, who afterwards became a Conservative, who had dined well if with insufficient wisdom. "I am," he said solemnly, "diagonally opposed to my honourable friend." Which was not what he meant at all. Upon another occasion, an otherwise dull discussion of a commercial treaty negotiated by Mr. Fielding with the French Government was enlivened by the comments of a country doctor from Ontario. He was a dear old man, an excellent host and companion, a competent fisherman and, I believe, an able physician. But he could not make speeches and there were certain resources of the English language with which he was unfamiliar. He attacked the Fielding treaty as menacing the health of Canada's men and women, the Canadian duties having been reduced to facilitate the entry and consumption of divers and sundry light French wines. "Mr. Speaker," said my friend, "the people of this country do not want these adulterous liquors." Then there was the Eastern Ontario Conservative member, a sincere and disappointed protectionist, who moved a former Parliament to tears by a heart-rending word picture of "all them tall chimneys layin' there dead." But by far the best example of these oratorical lapses, the gem of purest ray serene, was furnished by a British Columbian member whose recollection of the classics had become somewhat involved. "The Government," said this gentleman, "opened Pandora's box and out jumped the Trojan's horse." Even "the gentlemen of the Press"—favourite expression of Sir Robert Borden were sometimes caught napping. Not often, but once in a while. Laurier had a well-known fondness for the Bible as the source of the finest literature of any language. Orator that he was, he knew the value of a scriptural phrase in adorning his rich periods or his still more impressive perorations. He was once discussing his own or somebody's political misfortunes. The details have escaped my memory, but he had been back at the pages of his Bible, and he said, "The stars in their courses fought against Sissera." I think every man in the Gallery with one exception proceeded to inform the Canadian people that there had been some sort of stellar combination or cabal designed for the undoing of Cicero. If I avoided this error, it was because I had spent most of my boyhood in the front pew, and had suffered much.

I should like to mention one other member of a bygone Parliament, Edward Norman Lewis, who hailed from Goderich, Ontario, where the late Dan McGillicuddy once published his *Signal*. Lewis was something of a pioneer, including the matter of personal apparel. He was addicted to neckties of the most blatant flaring red I ever saw. He it was who tried to convince the Canadian Parliament of the advantages of daylight-saving, or summer time, when advanced time was still in its early experimental stage in a very few, very scattered and very bold communities. The House of Commons, which had certain well-established Bourbon traits, laughed him to scorn. At another time this same Lewis proposed that Canada should establish an attaché at Washington, another unheard of departure. Laurier would have none of it. "We are getting on," he said, "very well as we are," or words to that effect. The Huron member was put in his place. Now we have our ambassador at Washington, another in Tokyo—of all places—another in Paris, and we are about to send one to the Netherlands. Up to the moment a few places, such as Timbuctoo, Lhassa, etc., have been overlooked, if not neglected, but we have not yet got into our stride.

· · · · · ·

Parliament sometimes left the capital as when it, or most of it, journeyed to Peterborough, Ontario, in July, 1904, for the official opening of the newly-built liftlock, which was considered then as it is now a triumph of engineering skill, and then as now a very costly addition to a useless canal system. The Trent Canal ranks high among this country's many examples of political profligacy and administrative imbecility. I suppose the liftlock moves an occasional motor-boat up, or takes a canoe down, but it can do very little more. Its opening, however, was a great event and the gathering of peculiar-looking people here reproduced attests the interest that was taken in it and perhaps the hopes that were entertained of it. In the centre of the front row are to be seen the Honourable A. G. Blair, former Minister of Railways, the Honourable H. R. Emmerson, and the distinguished engineer, Collingwood Schrieber. Immediately back of them are Postmaster-General Mulock and Senator George A. Cox. Elsewhere may be found Major Sam Hughes, Senator George McHugh, Senator Watson, Walter Scott, M.P., Archie Campbell, M.P., Senator William Gibson, and Senator Ross. The millinery of both genders express the period's most advanced modes as well as the more conservative models purveyed in Lakefield and Peterborough.

Upon another occasion, a good while after, we went down by special train to Halifax and to the old wooden Church of St. Paul's, to bury the last of the Fathers of Confederation, Sir Charles Tupper. It was a wet journey, the mourners drowning their grief with Spartan fortitude. Sometimes the Press Gallery went away alone, or with a few carefully selected members of the House, perhaps even of the Senate, one of these jaunts taking us up to the top of Lake Temiskaming, with stops at Haileybury and New Liskeard. This happened in the early days of the Cobalt boom, but if there was fortune there we knew nothing of it and passed it by. At times also the Gallery would entertain an angel unawares. It did this once with a newspaperman from Minneapolis, a very modest, friendly sort of fellow, and we

bestirred ourselves to make him feel at home.   In
the matter of hospitality our facilities were limited
and our resources small, but our hearts were of gold,
and we said to this visitor, at one of the later stages
of the evening, "Have you ever tasted a John
Collins?" He replied in the expectant negative
and appeared suitably conscious of what was in
fact, or would have been, a lamentable ignorance.
We then said to him, "Come with us and we will
round out your education and fill you with joy."
The trouble began when he accepted. He manifested a marked affection for the exhilarating
beverage. We thought it was a case of love at first
sight and prided ourselves and preened ourselves on
having shown this American something of the
greater world. But he kept on drinking John
Collinses and we, perforce, trailed along with him.
We were showing him, introducing him, etc. We
did our best, but it was not good enough. When
the initiation ceremonies came at last to an end,
our visitor was still looking rather hopefully in the
direction of the bar, while the rest of us were gazing
up with glassy eyes toward the underside of the
table at which we had been sitting. The next day,
or it may have been two or three days later—I think
probably it was—I decided to fathom this mystery.
"Jermane," said I, "speaking as man to man, and
not for publication, is it a fact that you had never
tasted a John Collins?" "Oh, no," he answered
brightly, "only over there we call it a Horse's
Neck." There are times when one goes away
sorrowful. The adventure had cost us a lot of
money, some profound and protracted physical

disturbances, and upon these had now been superimposed a realization of having been sold down
the river; it was humiliation at its worst.

. . . . .

There were in the Laurier Cabinet a number of
ministers who were reputed to be much more
catholic in their personal pursuits than in their
politics. The tales which were bandied about by
scandal-mongers, a term which in this instance would
have to include the entire adult population of the
Capital, would have made a new *Decameron*. Of
course there was more smoke than fire, but there
was good reason to believe now and then that something was burning. A Fredericton newspaper
attacked the then Minister of Railways, Honourable
Henry Emmerson, who informed Parliament of his
intention to do battle with the beasts at Ephesus.
A lawsuit was launched, and in due course came to
trial in the New Brunswick capital. It did not get
very far, the plaintiff entering a *nolle prosequi*, or
something of the kind, which was, of course, a victory
for the defendant. That bright newspaperman and
excellent companion, Tom King, then of the Toronto
World, telegraphed his newspaper that Mr. Emmerson had left the city with the beasts of Ephesus in
hot pursuit. The trial having ended, most of the
counsel and newspaper men proceeded to Saint
John by boat, in the company of some eminent
provincial Liberals. On the way down, the captain
was obliged to stop his steamer to permit the passage
of two cow moose which were leisurely swimming
across the river. One of our company, being versed
in venery, undertook to explain the method of

attracting the bull moose by imitating the call of the cow. "Ah," said King, "how effective that would be in summoning ministers into a division."

I have always deprecated this method of playing upon the natural inclinations of a bull moose. It isn't cricket. The hunter, armed with an under-sized megaphone, succeeds in making a noise very like that of a cow moose of exceptionally friendly disposition. The distant bull, without pausing to reflect upon the forwardness of the female, comes rampaging through the bush full of high domestic resolve, only to experience the bitterest kind of disappointment and disillusionment. There could be no greater contrast between the anticipation and the actual reception. Instead of a compliant cow, there is a hunter with a high-powered rifle. The only comforting aspect of the episode is that the bull seldom lives long enough to meditate upon the full extent of the treachery that has been his undoing. Mr. Emmerson left the cabinet soon after.

.   .   .   .

The Laurier Government staggered in 1905 and regained its balance with considerable difficulty; also without Sir Clifford Sifton. For four or five years previously the people of the North-West Territories, through their political leaders, had been agitating for provincial status. Growing pains were generally prevalent in Canada, and the West had them. The real or main object, probably, was to secure control of the lands and other natural resources, and ironically enough, that object was not realized until long after. In other words, the Territories got what they wanted least, and they very nearly got an ecclesiastical school system into the bargain.

In the recorded and unrecorded history of this unlovely political chapter there is no evidence that those who asked for provincial autonomy had given anything more than a passing thought to the question of education. Nor is there any evidence that those members of the Federal Government, who were party to the final negotiations and to the framing of the Autonomy Bills, ever hinted and much less suggested to the prairie representatives that education would be an issue. In point of fact, the Western spokesmen had this school question sprung upon them. It dismayed them, they had no reason to expect that the Laurier who had swept into power on the crest of a national protest against the attempt of the ill-starred Tupper Government to coerce the Province of Manitoba in 1896, would come forward in 1905 with a measure deliberately designed to fasten a clerical school system, not upon the Territories, but upon the provinces that were to be carved out of them. The Church, however, had been active, and it was altogether probable that the political legerdemain which had succeeded in 1896 would not have succeeded nine years later. Be that as it may, the introduction of the Autonomy Bills at the beginning of February precipitated a major parliamentary crisis and shook the country with the violence which only a religious controversy can exert. Constitutional pundits argued this way and that, overhauled the British North America Act, examined and re-examined the educational ordinances passed by the territorial legislature and the original authority of the legislature in school matters, not only as defined but as intended by those who gave the North-West its first administrative machinery.

This practice of interpreting the motives and objects of men long dead and gone is still in favour. There are eminent parliamentarians now who are industriously engaged in telling the people of Canada, not what the constitutional law is, but what the Fathers of Confederation intended it to be. It does not occur to them that the aims of these Fathers are in the law, and that the men who framed the British North America Act were not an aggregation of illiterates incapable of expressing their design in understandable legal terminology. In 1905, it did not matter to the Orangemen of Ontario, or the Protestant clergy throughout the country, what the Mackenzie Government had or had not meant to do in the field of territorial education. What did matter was that Parliament was being required to enact legislation which would start two new provinces on their way, bound hand and foot to an educational system devised by the Dominion Government, and from which they could never hope to escape.

Public opinion at times like these is inclined to confine itself to rather bald facts, and in this instance the issue was plain enough. For weeks the storm raged. Meetings were held, deputations were sent, protests were registered and newspapers all over the Dominion discharged editorial broadsides in every issue. The Borden Opposition, not unnaturally, took the side of the fence which the Laurier Government had vacated, and the party which, officially at any rate, had endeavoured to jam a

separate school system down the unwilling throats
of the people of Manitoba, now proclaimed the
unviolable sanctity of provincial rights and Mr.
Borden stood foursquare "upon the rock of the
Constitution." With that unmoveable object under
him, he offered an amendment which was in substance that the two new provinces of Saskatchewan
and Alberta should be left to their own educational
devices.

It so happened that when Laurier elected to
plunge the country into this steamy turmoil, two of
his most important ministers were away, Mr.
Fielding and Mr. Sifton. The Opposition, not
altogether lacking in intelligence, drew attention to
this circumstance and did not fail to suggest that
the two absent ministers were not in accord with the
Government policy. There is plenty of good reason
to believe that they were not, though the sentiments
of the Minister of Finance, when he returned, were
less definitely proclaimed than were those of the
Minister of the Interior. Sifton resigned. Behind
him were the Western Liberal members and things
were not looking any too bright. It began to be
whispered abroad that Laurier would compromise.
It began, also, to be whispered, even to be stated
boldly and in print, that the Government was
endeavouring to hold the support of its Western
wing by liberal promises of preferment. Laurier
did compromise. Fielding accepted his concessions
for one set of reasons and Sifton for another, and the
Western Liberals fell into line. It was probably
nothing more than a coincidence that so many of
these Western Liberals, at intervals thereafter, either
found promotion in the House or drifted quietly

away to the Senate, to the Bench, or to high provincial office—only the coincidence had been predicted.

Laurier had gone to the country in 1904 and returned triumphant. The election of 1904, by the way, had brought into the House of Commons a reasonably young Quebec lawyer, one Ernest Lapointe, who had been elected in Kamouraska, succeeding the Honourable H. G. Carroll, Solicitor-General, who had gone to the Bench, later to become Lieutenant-Governor of Quebec. The newcomer made no impression on the House. In appearance he was large, well-nourished and inactive. He was one of those disconcerting examples of hidden mobility, hidden energy, and hidden ambition. He knew no English. He set to work to remove this handicap and succeeded so well as to be able to participate in an astonishingly short time in English as well as in French debates. Parliament began to sit up and take notice of him. He has been in the House ever since, moving in 1919 to the old Laurier seat of Quebec East, and he has proved in every respect a worthy successor to the great Liberal leader. He is Canada's Minister of Justice, a master of both languages, an orator of outstanding ability, a lawyer of acknowledged eminence, a man respected and beloved. His name is to be found on sundry of this country's treaties and he has executed important international commissions for the Dominion, always with credit to his country and himself.

7

Behind the Reciprocity Stage

Again, in 1908, Laurier tested his popularity and history repeated itself, but I think that election marked the beginning of the end. The popular vote was very close, but there was another and more important consideration, namely, new blood in the Opposition. Nor was it merely new blood. It was red and flowed vigorously. There were new Conservative members appearing in the House after that election who were to become cabinet ministers and one of them was destined for the highest office of all. This was Arthur E. Meighen, B.A., who had captured a Liberal seat in Portage la Prairie. He appeared to have an analytical mind, to be disconcertingly industrious, and to have speaking talents of no mean order. "Borden," Laurier is reported to

P.P.T.—9

have said, "has found a man." But Arthur
Meighen, if the most outstanding, was by no means
the only effective debater who entered the lists at
that time, and among the others were men who
positively refused to stand uncovered at the Laurier
shrine, much less to kneel before it.

One of the most valuable political assets of the
Liberal party up to then had been the creation and
careful preservation of a tradition that, whatever
storms might rage, the Opposition lightning should
never be loosed against the Liberal leader personally.
Sir Wilfrid was clothed with an artificial immunity
which depended wholly upon the willingness of the
Opposition to respect it, and in previous sessions it
had been respected. Some of these new men, however, were political atheists. They saw no good
reason for this reverence and they were shrewd
enough to realize that it placed the Opposition at a
serious disadvantage. They would have none of it.
They attacked the liberal idol, greatly to his surprise and to the dismay and discomfort of his
supporters. It was not a very noticeable thing even
at the time, but it destroyed a shibboleth and
altered the tone of debate and the whole atmosphere
of Parliament. On the occasion when a stuttering
Conservative from British Columbia referred to the
Liberal leader as a woolly aphis, the blasting
significance of the epithet was not immediately
appreciated. Laurier appeared to think that he
had received a compliment, a flattering illusion
which was dispelled upon subsequent consultation
of the dictionary.

Between 1908 and the Liberal catastrophe of
1911 there were signs that Laurier was a waning

star. He was still revered by his own followers and his Government was outwardly strong; but an illusion had been broken by very rude and unpleasant persons who obstinately refused to conduct their political combats according to the rules of their opponents.

Nevertheless, when the Conservative party was given its great opportunity in 1911, it very, very nearly threw the chance away. I went to Washington early in the reciprocity negotiations and remained there until the agreement was signed. It was not an easy assignment for a newspaper correspondent, since the conversations were conducted in profound secrecy. Fielding was there as the principal representative of the Canadian Government. We, I am speaking of the little group of Canadian newspapermen present, could get nothing out of him. Knowing him of old, I did not try. We talked to Philander Knox, the United States Secretary of State, and were treated with the utmost civility, but got no information—which was what most of us expected. We attended one of President Taft's afternoon press receptions at the White House where that most genial and joyous statesman sat at the head of a long table and heaved with merriment as one journalist after another— Americans mostly—hurled officially unanswerable and therefore improper questions at his head. We went to the Capital and conversed there with Sereno Elisha Payne, joint author of the Payne-Aldrich tariff, and he was slightly helpful, though unconsciously so. We went to the Commerce Department and collected Blue Books on trade with Canada. We studied the tariffs of the two countries.

When a Canadian or an American industrialist slipped unobtrusively into Washington and endeavoured to conceal himself in an upper room of the Willard or the Shoreham, or elsewhere, we smoked him out and, as a rule, we found out quite a lot from what he did not say. We got something of this industry and something on that and by the time plenipotentiaries had signed on the dotted line we had covered the ground pretty thoroughly.

At this time the Sixty-First Congress was in its Third Session, and noteworthy figures were marching up and down the stages of the two Houses. Oscar W. Underwood of Alabama was the most active Democrat in the House of Representatives and was later on to write the tariff which bore his name. Uncle Joe Cannon, he of the white chin-whisker, the big cigar and the black felt hat, was serving in his eighteenth Congress and was for the fourth time Speaker of the House. And among the members was that exuberant Democrat, Champ Clark of Bowling Green, Missouri, who did yeoman service in helping to bring about the defeat of the trade agreement. Nothing, of course, was farther from his intention, but he was one of those gentlemen in whom the tongue operates somewhat in advance of the intellect. Rising in his place in the House, he offered his support to the trade enterprise coupled with a loudly expressed hope that "I will live to see the day when the Stars and Stripes will fly clear from the North Pole to the Rio Grande." It was with a certain degree of pleasure that correspondents of Canadian Conservative newspapers telegraphed this useful pronouncement verbatim to their home offices. It did wonders.

The Sixty-First Congress has never been equalled by any of its successors in one respect, namely, its senatorial ·distinction. There were many men in the Upper House whose names have gone into the history of the United States. They were outstanding in a generation which was rich in the character of its public men. There were veterans of the Civil War, such as Colonel Henry Dupont of Delaware— hero of Fortress Munroe and Cedar Creek; James P. Taliaferro of Florida, and Bacon of Georgia, whose parents, scorning to call him either Francis or Roger, had gone to Imperial Rome for inspiration and had thereby achieved a super-success by christening him Augustus Octavius. Not many members of that Senate, perhaps, are now living, though some are well remembered. William Borah was there from Idaho, and was doing pretty much the same then as he did since, that is to say, he kept in the political limelight without ever doing anything constructive. Borah belonged to that numerically impressive company of men who are fatally handicapped in their inability to rise above themselves. Among those who have gone the long road beside Borah are Chauncey Depew and Elihu Root of New York, both men of great eminence in their day. Chauncey Depew, railroad magnate, formal orator and after-dinner wit, was reputed the best post-prandial speaker in the United States, and it was the custom, as so often happens—sometimes in the case of a movie actress—to attribute to him spritely anecdotes of which he was not the legitimate parent. It was not necessary that he busy himself overmuch as a senator since he was highly decorative as well as brilliant and had a formidable industrial background. He looked the statesman, without being anything of the kind, or pretending to be, and was exactly the right senatorial spokesman for the Empire State. Had he not been the official orator at the unveiling of the Statue of Liberty? Root was different, perhaps abler, certainly more serious. A lawyer of international reputation, he was a man of high character and exceptionable culture, and it was said that so unusual were his qualities of mind and so correct was his spiritual outlook that he could never become President of the United States. He was one of the men, by the way, who represented the Republic on the Alaskan Boundary Commission.

Robert La Follette, still a Republican but still independent, was finishing his term as Senator for Wisconsin; Read Smoot was there from Utah. He was joint author of the Hawley-Smoot Tariff. And very prominent in this company was Henry Cabot Lodge of Massachusetts. He was one of the Lodges so long and so intimately associated with the "home of the bean and the cod," one of the family who spoke only to Lowells, while the latter, as you all know, were still more rigidly exclusive in their social contacts. Henry Cabot Lodge himself seemed curiously out of place in a political assembly. He was a man of letters, had demonstrated a marvellous fertility as a producer of books and was wont to give literature as his profession. Nevertheless, he played active parts in at least two national Republican conventions and was about as thoroughgoing a party-man as could be found even in the New England of a quarter of a century ago. He, too, had been an Alaskan Boundary Commissioner. I recall, also, Gore, the blind senator from Oklahoma, and, with diminished pleasure, the "Boy-Orator," Albert J. Beveridge of Indiana, who spoke with a painful intensity and deliberation. He did what other rockets do after they have finished going up.

In between whiles we visited what are called in the guide books points of interest—the Arlington Military Cemetery, Washington's home at Mt. Vernon, old Alexandria, the little house where Lincoln died, the navy yard, and Annapolis. Naturally we saw the monuments. There is one in the Capitol, endowing the late John Hancock with a marble immortality. Hancock, as you are aware, was one of the fathers of the Republic, the first to put his name to the Declaration of Independence, that document which was, and is, intended to convey the impression that America is a free country. There is not a citizen in the United States now who would not be willing to part with a good deal of inflated money in order to have his name on that historic charter, but we can well imagine that John Hancock had to think twice about it and that his associates were thinking three and possibly four times. It was a momentous step, because if things went wrong, and it was by no means impossible that they would go wrong, a signature to that declaration would be a death warrant. The difference between a patriot and a traitor is a difference in the point of view and for practical purposes the accuracy of the appellation is determined by the whim of the dice. It is not difficult even at this late date to visualize the little company contemplating the Jeffersonian masterpiece and each preferring to sign somewhere down near the bottom. Somebody had to break the ice, and John Hancock, with high courage and probably deep misgivings, "wrote his name where all nations should behold it and where all time should not efface it." At any rate, that is what an admiring sculptor has chiselled into this memorial. The fact of the matter is that it was a very near thing. Hancock would have fared very badly indeed if the British had caught him, and Gage had done his best to catch him on that memorable march to Lexington and Concord. This, you will recall, was the occasion of Paul Revere's ride, the general ringing of bells, and other occurrences by reason of which Gage found himself marching through a country alarmed and ready, and the Hancock bird had flown.

Sir George Perley had asked me to collect what material I could in Washington for the use of the Conservative party, although the leaders of that party had not yet seen the light, and I took back with me such data as I thought would help. As I have said, the ball being at the Conservatives' feet, they were nearly all for kicking it away. The Liberal party, as represented in Ottawa, welcomed the Reciprocity Agreement as a gift from God. The Conservatives were caught in the flood of a general jubilation. Outside the capital, some Conservative newspapers were praising the agreement with very faint damns and some of them giving it out and out approval.

There was a dangerously long period of indecision, of veering in this direction and that. Party leaders stood shivering on the brink and required a great deal of urging before they could be induced to take the plunge. The reasons for this were, partly the first wave of approval which had greeted the reciprocity proposal, and, to a lesser extent, the question of consistency. Could the party oppose this pact in view of its own political record? Counsel was sought and obtained from Conservative leaders in provincial fields and these assembled in Ottawa for what proved to be vital deliberations. My own impression was and still is that these men from the outer marches had much to do in turning the scale of party opinion, their influence being strengthened by growing restiveness throughout the country.

The Conservative press, after some initial wobbling, became virtually unanimous in condemnation of the agreement. Borden himself was free. He had left the Liberal party on the unrestricted reciprocity issue twenty years before. Prominent Liberals were breaking away. A very noteworthy development, and one that should have warned the government, was the publication of the famous manifesto bearing the signatures of eighteen leading Liberals of Toronto setting forth ten reasons why the agreement should not be ratified. One of these Liberals was W. T. White, vice-president and general manager of the National Trust Company, and it was this issue that brought into the Conservative party one of its most eminent members and later into the Conservative Government a minister who was to make Canadian history. When the Conservative party finally made up its mind to fight the pact with all its resources, and with the promise of formidable Liberal backing, the end of the long Laurier régime was decreed. Thereafter there were no half measures, no hesitations, no attempts to compromise. Borden himself showed impressive qualities of leadership in the course of the campaign which followed. Among his most active captains were men who in previous years had worked with Laurier or had supported him through good report, and ill. The election became a national demonstration, and its outcome inevitable.

It is possible and perhaps probable that had Laurier gone to the country immediately, that is to say, before the agreement had been studied and its defects exposed, he might have won, in which event the subsequent history of Canada, and more especially of that glorious and bloody chapter which included the World War, would have been written by other hands and in another ink. But for the first time the political instinct of the great Liberal leader was at fault. I believe that he was badly advised and that the author of the advice is still living. Be that as it may, he waited, and the longer he delayed, the greater was the certainty of his defeat. The Conservative Opposition, armed with powerful arguments, was fighting the agreement on the floor of the House. Liberals of high position in different parts of the country were forsaking their party and making common cause with the Opposition, and when the Government finally decided to go to the country it faced a thoroughly aroused and hostile public opinion. I remember standing outside the Council Chamber in the East Block when Mr. Fielding came out from that fateful cabinet meeting, tired and anxious-looking. He said simply, "Parliament is dissolved." I got a little scoop out of it.

It was a fierce campaign, but the Government had already lost the fight. Sir Clifford Sifton had thrown his influence to the Conservatives and was employing his great organizing ability in their behalf. I stood beside Sir Wilfrid Laurier on the night of September 21, 1911, in the ancient Marché Ste. Pierre, in the city of Quebec, while the election returns were coming in. The place was badly lighted and full of shadows, and full of fear. Laurier, I believe, had been nominated in this hall, in 1878, after his defeat on going back to Drummond and Arthabaska as newly-appointed Minister of Inland Revenue in the Mackenzie Government. I don't know why he was back there on this momentous night unless he yielded to some homing instinct. None of his ministers was with him, only an anxious and, as the night wore on, a dumbly sympathetic and very mournful gathering of his old constituents. It was the hour of his Gethsemane, but I will say this, that no man could have stood more proudly under so terrible a stroke. His reign was over. He went away and one by one, or in little silent groups, his followers, stunned and puzzled, passed slowly out of a darkened hall.

The following notes from the Toronto *Telegram* of September 22, 1911, depict this memorable scene in part as it appeared to me then.

Standing before his own constituents of Quebec East, in a hot, badly-lighted and evil-smelling top storey of the old St. Peter's Market, Sir Wilfrid Laurier acknowledged his defeat. It must be said of him, that after all, he did it as became a man. It was the hardest thing he ever had to do—a thing that he had never thought to do. He had gone more confidently into this election than into any other of his long career. He stood last night a proud, pathetic figure, his power gone, his government a wreck, and spoke the word that he had never thought to speak. He spoke it to a people who, for more than a quarter of a century, had blindly followed him, believing him unbeatable, and now they looked upon a new Laurier. "Le Vieux Coq" still, but no longer the dictator of a government backed by a majority of nearly half a hundred.

They saw before them an old man, who was telling them a strange story. He had told them a few days before that the weapon had not been fashioned that would bring him down. He told them now that he had failed; they cheered him and he went miserably away. Liberals have said that "Laurier will never be beaten." Sir Wilfrid Laurier believed it. Laurier's luck had been a by-word among politicians. It was because of this that many Liberals in the last parliament supported reciprocity, who otherwise would have fought it with all their energy. They thought that "Laurier can get away with anything"—and they acted accordingly. Laurier believed it up till seven and eight o'clock last evening.

The story of the election was late in getting to Quebec. It gave the Liberals a longer period of hope. Nor did the first returns tell the story, and when Sir Wilfrid left his hotel he was still confident and sure. He was ready to joke about Toronto. "Reciprocity," he said to the *Telegram*, "hasn't done much there." He was still sure of Ontario, the first list of losses only drawing from him the comment that "Ontario is not doing very well."

But at St. Peter's Market the operation of counting the losses had not proceeded far before the possible defeat of the Government was made manifest. Out in the street the crowd was good-naturedly applauding the election of W. F. Maclean in South York. Inside there was also a chance to cheer. Laurier had won Soulanges against Dr. Lortie. Out in the street the crowd applauded the bulletin announcing the election of Colonel Sam Hughes in Victoria and Haliburton; inside the loss of Labelle was being received in painful silence. Thereafter the Cabinet was losing ministers every few minutes and when the ticker showed an election in Brome, and the name wasn't Fisher, Sir Wilfrid got up. By this time the crowd in the hall knew pretty well what was coming. They cheered their member. He had come to them in '78, wanting to be taken in, and they had had him ever since. They gave him a cheer, and closed in towards the platform the better to hear. Sir Wilfrid spoke briefly, perhaps being unwilling to trust himself too far, then sat down at the table with the look of a man who has said good-bye.

Only in Quebec was reciprocity a minor issue. There the Conservatives had the advantage of an unnatural alliance with the Nationalists led by Henri Bourassa. These Nationalists were not keen either for or against reciprocity, but they were anti-Imperialistic, heatedly so, and they disliked the Laurier naval policy as being too British. The Conservative party, with all its traditional Imperialism, nevertheless found this alliance convenient. There was no bargain, or, if there was, I heard nothing of it either then or since, and the so-called Nationalist ministers in the Borden Government had always been Conservatives. The Nationalists campaigned in their own way and added materially to the gaiety of nations. Here is an account of one of their political excursions which I attended. It is substantially as written then, for consumption by Toronto *Telegram* readers.

Another political "joy-ride." You find your way to the old Bonaventure station of the Grand Trunk in Montreal at mid-day Sunday. You allow yourself to be swallowed up in a rushing mass of exuberant French-Canadian humanity, mostly young, but not all; mostly male, but not all. The mass is arrayed in its Sunday clothes, the same being also its holiday clothes, for Sunday afternoon in French-Canadian Quebec is, first and last and above all, a holiday. The clothes do not always harmonize. There are watch chains heavy enough to tow a liner, and the neckties resemble chunks from a Turner landscape. But these little things don't matter.

,   The mass pours itself—and you—into a collection of more or less up-to-date railway coaches. It is a special train. They are all specials hereabouts and nowadays. If a special won't do, they get an extra special. This particular special has been bespoken by the Nationalist Club, which, as everybody knows, is the Bourassa Club. It is a train of eight cars, and at half-past twelve the eight cars are bulging with joyously excited Nationalists, who shout "*Vive* Bourassa," and thereupon laugh consumedly, as if it were the richest thing in the world. And for the time being so it is.

It is a great thing in Quebec these days to shout "Hoora Bourassa," and have the elder of the village stare at you, in a lurking fear of speedy judgment. But, and this by way of variety only, a Nationalist will shout, "Hoora, Laurier." Then everybody laughs. And therein is the astounding change. The day has come when it is to laugh at the name of Laurier in Quebec. "Le Vieux Coq" may get his votes on the 21st, but to the old chantecler of the Liberal party there is, and can be, no recompense for the laugh on the lips of his native province. I watched Sir Wilfrid go out from the dining hall of the Windsor Sunday night with Madame upon his arm. He looks very much an old man, and weary.

The special train in due time snorts and coughs and splutters its way out of the station and over the Victoria Bridge. At St. Henry, more crowds of Nationalists squeeze in, and at St. Lambert there are others, each additional regiment being greeted with shouts of ecstatic welcome. "*Vive* Bourassa," says one, and "*Vive* Bourassa," say the others. The younger Nationalists then light cigarettes, while the older ones produce venerable pipes, out of which they blow clouds of smoke of *tabac Canadien*, the aroma of which some people are said to enjoy. They adorn themselves with badges, and on each badge is the face of Bourassa.

They pass around little dodgers, on which there are verses entitled "O Bourassa." The verses are to be sung to the air of "O Canada." The mass sings them in conflicting keys and rapidly varying volume. To the listener it is melancholy. To the performer it is clearly a treat above the common kind. "O Bourassa," they sing, assuring all concerned that Bourassa is a hero and valiant "soldier."

So it goes. The special rolls fussily out into the country, passing by a long succession of level pastures, stretching away to the river. The hay is there, stacks of it; the hay which tends to send reciprocity running almost neck and neck with *"la marine de la guerre"* in Quebec. Also the horses. They are plentiful, and the colts are seen galloping away from the Nationalist special and the war cry of *"Vive* Bourassa!" Even special trains on present missions eventually get somewhere. This does. It pulls up at Laprairie, all out of breath, and lets out a whistle of relief.

Laprairie is not a large or imposing place, whatever may be said of its inhabitants. It is, however, the most get-at-able point in the riding of Laprairie-Napierville, and hence its visitants. This riding is, or has been, Liberal, the late member being one Lanctot (not Adelard). The worthy Lanctot is in danger of being run off his feet by Gustave Monette, a curly-haired young man, slender, eloquent, intensely earnest, sworn enemy of *la marine*— in short, a Nationalist of the Nationalists. He is a young Montreal lawyer, aged twenty-four. Laprairie boasts of three things of considerable size, a brick-making plant, a Roman Catholic seminary of some sort, and a huge church, the chimes in which tower ring out as the invading army rushes up from the railway station through the village. The sober citizens of Laprairie appear to view these high doings with some inward concern, and they gather on the porches, galleries and steps, and gaze at the newcomers. Whereat the latter shout, "*Vive*

Bourassa,'' and rush on through winding streets, arched
over with weather-beaten willows.

By and by more invaders come. A special pants
up to the station from Hemmingford and emits five
hundred enthusiasts, who rush up through the quiet
streets of Laprairie like a boatload of baseball fans for
the Toronto Island stadium. By some marvellous
instinct, these visiting Nationalists know exactly where
to go. They never miss a turn, never enquire, and
never hesitate. You stay with them, and you get to the
place of battle. This time it is a huge lot, almost under
the shadow of the big church. At the back of the lot
there is an ancient structure, which might once have been
a driving shed.

Under the shed are to be observed lemonade booths
and pop emporiums, and just in front of, and adjacent to,
the shed is the platform. It rests upon four enormous
casks, which are empty. The platform is resplendent
with red, white and blue bunting, Union Jacks and the
tri-colour. To the left there is another shed, the roof
of which does duty as a grandstand. To the right, the
verandah of a residence is crowded with spectators and
listeners, conspicuous among whom is a group of priests.

The vacant lot is no longer vacant. It is packed
with people, and many are women. You see a man who
has brought his whole family, and a capacious basket.
It is a picnic. An automobile honks its way into the
crowd. There is a roar of acclaim. Bourassa has
arrived. More cheers, as he ascends the platform, the
same dapper man in the same grey suit, and the soft
grey hat, the close cropped head under the hat, the same
restless ambition in the head.

There is also on the platform Roch Lanctot, late
Liberal member for the riding of Laprairie-Napierville.
Mr. Lanctot has a plan. A little group of his supporters
in one corner of the crowd stands ready to help him out.
Lanctot demands that the meeting be an "*assemblée
contradictoire.*" He thinks that this will break the force
of the Bourassa appeal. Bourassa refuses it, or some one
does for him, whereupon Lanctot tells the crowd about

it, and subtly suggests that Henri Bourassa fears to meet him, a simple farmer, in joint debate. Loud groans from the Lanctot group. Then there arises Mr. E. Patenaude, local member, who is tall and fair and hoarse. He reminded the audience that, when Laurier came to the riding in the last campaign, Lanctot refused to have an *assemblée contradictoire.* (Great applause.)

But Mr. Patenaude is subjected to a series of interruptions from the Lanctot group. A large man, apparently combining the qualities of Messrs. Johnson and Gotch, is observed to detach himself from the crowd on the platform and disappear into the crowd below. A moment later there is a violent upheaval in the vicinity of the Lanctot's supporters. One of them is obviously getting his. The crowd begins to look like a whirlpool. The chief of police (who is also the police force) appears upon the scene. Quiet is restored. Gustave Monette gets to the front of the platform, attacks the navy, declines to declare himself as the follower of any one man, and gracefully skates over the reciprocity issue. The audience sees in this youthful candidate discretion beyond his years, and he is wildly cheered.

Bourassa begins his speech. He is vociferously welcomed. The *Bienvenue,* inscribed upon the banner above his head, becomes a cheer out of four thousand throats. Again the chimes ring out from the church tower. Bourassa does not miss this happy omen. He misses nothing. "It must be a young Nationalist who is being baptized," he says, and the applause is universal. The Nationalist leader says little that he has not said before. But he gets a little closer to a declaration of opinion on the question of reciprocity. He favours the opening of the United States markets, but he thinks that this could have been obtained in a little while, with no cost to Canada.

Another row in the vicinity of the Lanctot men. Bourassa turns it swiftly to account. "These interruptions," he says, "are a good sign that the Liberals are going to be beaten, because when the Liberals fought their battles on real principles, they had no need of paid drunken scoundrels to support them." Now, no man cares to be openly and publicly described as a paid drunken scoundrel, even at a Sunday afternoon political· meeting in Quebec. The interrupters stop interrupting. Mr. Bourassa gets on with his argument. He points out that some of the United States duties have already come down, a sure sign of what is to come, independent of Canada's action.

Then he talks hay to the farmer, telling him that not reciprocity but weather regulates the price of hay, and will go on regulating it. He gets to the navy, and is in the middle of this favourite theme, when a voice says: "What about that $2,000 you never accounted for?" A somewhat pointed question, requiring an answer. Bourassa gives it. "My friend," he says, "I spent it in the service of my country, with the approval and at the express wish of Sir Wilfrid Laurier. Go and ask him if it's not so. If he tells you otherwise, then he is a perjurer in the high office which he holds." And so it went, on to an uproarious conclusion.

About this time or a little later I met Sir George Foster at the gates of the Parliament Buildings in Ottawa. It used to be said of him that he was not a practical politician. "What," I asked him, "are you going to do with these Nationalists after the election?" He wagged his beard at me. "Bilkey," he said solemnly, "one thing at a time."

A word as to the character, or at any rate, the characteristics of the Nationalist leader. I never succeeded in convincing myself of Henri Bourassa's sincerity. He is a spent force now, but in his heyday of thirty years ago, when he was a very sharp thorn in the sensitive side of the Liberal party, he was *par excellence un poseur.* Just as Mackenzie King is a grandson of William Lyon Mackenzie, and proud of his descent, so Bourassa capitalized, or sought to do, upon the fact that Louis Joseph Papineau was his grandfather. He sat in the tenth parliament as deputy for Labelle in which is situated the old Papineau home, Montebello. He chose to be an ardent and uncompromising apostle of nationalism. He had resigned from Parliament in 1899 as a protest against the sending of a Canadian expeditionary force to South Africa at the bidding, as he insisted, of the British Government, and he preached nationalism with consistent vigour until near the close of his public life. But I am mightily mistaken if much of this was not a garment.

Bourassa at the height of his influence in Quebec was also at the height of his vanity, a very lofty pinnacle, and I thought and still think that it was this vanity rather than a cause dear to his heart that he was attempting to serve. He was an excellent debater, dangerously logical and a master of the English tongue, but in Parliament at least he was never moving, a man without emotion and incapable of arousing emotion in others, except upon the hustings in Quebec. An egregious exhibitionist, it was his habit to enter the House of Commons, fold his arms upon the brass bar at the entrance, and gaze about him, and as he was no novelty in the Green Chamber, the irresistible inference was that he sought to engage the interest of the galleries. "Who is that man standing down there?" "Oh, that is Henri Bourassa, the famous nationalist leader."

Once, at the behest of the Toronto *Telegram*, I went to his office in *Le Devoir* Building for some first-hand information upon his political aspirations. I was received cordially enough; but the impression

I got, and the only one, was that of being regarded as a prospective vehicle for the wider dissemination of nationalist propaganda. Of course, the man was able, in some respects brilliant, and he always had followers, but he was never anything but a disturbing element and even his own little world in time grew tired of him. He accomplished nothing, nothing constructive, and, fortunately, nothing really destructive. He flared for a while and went out, not perhaps unhonoured, but certainly unsung.

8

New Government—and War

MONTREAL has always
been as religious as it is loyal, which is an understatement, and it did more for the Papal Legate in
September, 1910, than it had done for its future
King in 1901. It was the logical place for the
Twenty-Second Eucharistic Congress, held for the
first time in the Western Hemisphere. With its
preponderant French-Canadian population, Montreal ranked as the principal Roman Catholic city
in North America, and work done by Archbishop
Paul Bruchesi had been actively supported. St.
James Cathedral, which reproduces upon a more
modest scale the general architecture of the great
church of St. Peter's in Rome, became the centre of
the most remarkable religious demonstration ever
witnessed up to that time on this side of the Atlantic.

137

It was remarkable in its magnificence, in the number
of ecclesiastical dignitaries who participated and in
the extraordinary evidences of religious fervour
which marked its greater and its lesser ceremonies.

It brought to the Dominion a Special Papal
Legate, a very celebrated prince of the church, His
Eminence—and for this occasion His Excellency—
Cardinal Vincenzo Vannutelli. Vannutelli, who
ranked fourth in point of seniority in the Sacred
College, had earned his reputation as a diplomat of
the Vatican. He was high in the councils of the
Church, a man of seasoned judgment and deep
sagacity. He was tall, heavily built and rugged of
feature, but his face in repose was without expression, inscrutable, a bit suggestive of an Oriental
god. In his train came a great company of cardinals,
archbishops, bishops, priests, and Roman Catholic
laymen numbering some three hundred or more.
Many of the highest names in Roman Catholicism
were written on this memorable page.

The history of the Congress goes back to 1873
and to the French town of Paray-le-Monial, and
Montreal, not unnaturally, was stirred to its depths
—and be it known that the spiritual roots of this old
city lie a long way down and are very strong.
Pontifical masses were celebrated, impressive services were held in the Cathedral and in the historic
French church of Notre Dame. Messages were
received from His Majesty King George and from
His Holiness. There were some two hundred
thousand visitors milling about the city to see what
they could see. All these and all the people of
Montreal, who were not bed-ridden, lined the route
along which in the supreme moments of the Congress

passed the solemn procession of the Blessed Sacrament. As a spectacle it was unforgettable. The roads were strewn with flowers; towers and Venetian masts stood at intervals along the roadsides with pennants fluttering from them and with bunting and evergreens about them. The air was fragrant with incense. Forty to fifty thousand people, including one hundred and twenty-five cardinals, archbishops, bishops and other high ecclesiastical dignitaries, were slowly marching the long route to the high altar on Fletcher's Field. It took from four to four and a half hours for this vast procession to pass a given point.

Cardinal Vannutelli, carrying the Sacred Host from the altar of Notre Dame Church, was of course the central figure. He held the Eucharist aloft in a golden monstrance and walked bareheaded, wearing a golden cope. An enormous baldachino was carried over him, and it was gold. A majestic figure, this venerable prelate, carrying the Eucharist through all those hours while kneeling crowds of faithful Catholics devoutly crossed themselves. Before and after him in the richest trappings of clerical aristocracy and with the brilliant September sun shining down upon them, came the cardinals, archbishops, bishops, the lesser priests and the laymen who had journeyed from distant lands to witness this splendid spectacle and to be a part of it. I suppose that any good thing is right enough in its place and that this magnificent display served a useful purpose in furthering the missionary work of the Church, but I am wondering how many, if any, of the many thousands who saw the sacerdotal splendour of that day, who marvelled at the pomp and plumage of that proud procession, were minded to look backward through the mists, to stand along that Via Dolorosa along which a fainting outcast staggered with His Cross. And yet it seemed to me that there was one single link. Far down in the Montreal procession a brown-robed brother walked alone. He still marches in my memory. He looks neither to the right nor to the left, but only upon the road which his sandalled feet are treading; and he repeats incessantly, monotonously, but in a queer way impressively, four pregnant words, "*Le Cœur de Jesu—Le Cœur de Jesu—*"

Any one who undertakes to report a Eucharistic Congress for a Protestant newspaper circulating in a somewhat bigoted Orange community will find the experience more or less exacting. I contented myself, and have done so here, with describing a truly impressive procession, a very splendid spectacle it was, precisely as I saw it, but I am inclined to wonder how a General Bosquet might have adapted his Balaclava dictum, "*C'est magnifique mais ce n'est pas la guerre.*"

.   .   .   .   .   .

Those who have not witnessed the making of a Government have reason to be happier than those who have. It is a thoroughly unpleasant and discreditable business in which merit is disregarded, loyal service is without value, influence is the most important factor and geography and religion are important supplementary considerations.

The Borden Ministry was composed under standard conditions and was not, therefore, nearly as able, as honest, or as industrious an administrative aggregation as could have been had from the material available. Industrial and other magnates were present during the process of gestation, not, of course, in the public interest but in their own, which was quite a different thing. There were some broken hearts—in one instance, literally. In others, philosophy came to the rescue, but the pills were large and the swallowing was bitter. I met one aspirant in the rotunda of the Russell House, and he asked me who the ministers were to be. I told him as much as there was to tell and it was like striking a man down. There is some consolation in the reflection that this man subsequently rose to a very high place in the national life over another route and is still living.

I saw Andrew Broder of Dundas going heavily away from the office in which the cabinet was being made. He had earned the position of Minister of Agriculture, but the cards were dealt against him. A practical farmer and a very shrewd politician, Andrew Broder might not have made a very capable administrator, but the farmers could never have quarrelled with him and the new Government would have had in him an impregnable bulwark in an otherwise highly exposed position. Broder it was who, when an infant in arms bellowed at a public meeting and some one protested, declared that the cry of a child should be the national anthem of Canada.

I am sure that Lancaster of Lincoln never had the remotest suspicion that the railway portfolio would go to any one but himself. For many years he had occupied the rôle of railway critic and had crusaded, more or less successfully, for the protection of level crossings in the interests of four-footed and other cattle. He was known as "Cattleguard Lancaster," and he had referred so often to "thickly-peopled portions of cities, towns and villages" that in time he had succeeded in making one word of it. He might have made an efficient minister. These were some of the men who had nothing better than records of great industry and devoted party and public service to recommend them.

I think that Sir Robert Borden did the best he could in a very difficult situation, but his hands were not free, nor can the hands of any man similarly placed ever be free so long as public opinion continues to demand ministerial representation on bases which have nothing whatever to do with past or prospective usefulness.

The final draft of the new Ministry was crossed and dotted at the Borden residence, and I waited there for it. The list was brought to me by Sir Robert's secretary, and I looked at it. Blount was always a reader of expressions. He asked, "What's the matter with it?" The answer came from my soul's depths: "I hate to send the damn' thing."

Yet, as I have said, Borden did as well probably as most other men in his circumstances would, or could have done. There can be no doubt that great pressure was put upon him, pressure which even a much more resolute man would have found trouble in resisting. I am sure, too, that at this time Borden underestimated his own strength and that of the position to which he had been called.

. . . . . .

One of the achievements of the Borden Government was the establishment of parcel post throughout Canada. I was at that time resident correspondent of the Toronto *Mail and Empire*, and in that capacity it was my privilege to send the first non-official parcel to be transmitted from any point in Canada under this new system. Naturally it was necessary to secure permission from the then Postmaster-General, the Honourable Louis Philippe Pelletier. This man had been a brilliant student in his college days, had practised law at Quebec, had served in two provincial administrations, and had entered the Borden ministry on its formation. He was exceptionally clever, very highly strung, but imperfectly broken to political harness. He shone with spectacular radiance at Ottawa for a while, and then went out. In the meantime he had given us parcel post and, more particularly, had given me the first use of it. I conspired with him in his apartment while Madame rolled the cigarettes, which he smoked feverishly and incessantly. The object which I selected for mailing was a framed photograph of the minister himself, and I have always prided myself upon having been very subtle in enlisting his official co-operation by this means. The photograph appeared upon the front page of the *Mail and Empire*, frame and all. I am afraid it was rather a cheap frame.

. . . . . .

How many people recall the great naval debate of the winter of 1912 and 1913, a debate which made parliamentary history?

Things were looking rather bad in Europe in 1911

and worse in 1912.   European history in this respect has a way of repeating itself.

The only man who ever really understood the people of Europe was a Corsican.   The disturbing element in 1912 was the German Kaiser.   The German fleet was being augmented and Great Britain, alarmed and wary, was following suit. New Zealand was offering the Mother Country a dreadnought.   Australia was launching its second and third warships, and Winston Churchill, as First Lord of the Admiralty, was saying that "the gaps should be filled."   Canada was a gap with a naval establishment consisting of two training ships whose maintenance was costing the country a little less than two millions a year.   The Empire was being told that its bread routes must be protected.   Mr. Borden and some of his colleagues went to England and straightway became immersed in this atmosphere.   They returned to Canada with a naval policy which was to raise the most violent parliamentary storm ever witnessed before or since and was to divide public opinion into two frantically opposing schools.   Before the Government announced its policy, a conference between the Conservative and Liberal leaders was suggested, but Laurier was not to be drawn and, later, when the proposal that Canada should contribute three ships to the British navy was definitely before the country, he condemned the project as un-Canadian and he continued to fight the legislation tooth and nail through all its stages.

Briefly, the Conservative plan was to finance the construction of three vessels, to be among the most powerful in the world and to place them at the disposal of the British navy, but with a string on them. They could be recalled later to be used as units of a Canadian navy, if and when. . . . It will be seen from this reservation that the policy was not inconsistent with the Liberal position that Canada should have a navy of her own. It was thought at the time that the then remote possibility of a Canadian naval force scarcely sufficed to meet the requirements of what was declared to be an Empire emergency. The construction of three ships by the Dominion would meet those requirements. The Liberal Opposition, however, got around the difficulty quite simply and easily. They said there wasn't any emergency. The British Government and the British Admiralty thought otherwise, and Mr. Churchill had invited Canada to provide a "certain number of the largest and strongest ships of war which science can build or money supply." This invitation came at the end of a long Admiralty memorandum which proved to be a bone of fierce contention in the House of Commons, as most of Mr. Churchill's documentary production have always done everywhere.

The three ships never went into action because they were never built. The Opposition held up the legislation week by week, offered alternative proposals, and comforted itself with the mistaken belief that the Prime Minister would not or could not have recourse to strong measures. At one stage the House was kept in continuous session day and night for two weeks, Sundays excepted. Members slept in their seats. One of them, I remember, brought a pillow with him and bedded down. He was afterwards knighted but I think for some other reason.

Things happened during this protracted sitting, as, for example, when Dr. Michael Clark of Red Deer was named by the Speaker.   Up to that time it had been a generally accepted belief that to be named by the Speaker would be a most frightful experience, would shake the entire Parliamentary fabric to its foundations and would probably result in the summary ejection of the offending member and his more or less permanent incarceration with ball and chain by the Sergeant-at-Arms.   Dr. Clark, better known as Red Michael, had not been reared among these dismal apprehensions.   He had come from the north of England to ranch in Alberta, was a graduate of Edinburgh University, a brilliant speaker and the only uncompromising free-trader in the Parliament of his day.   On this occasion he was tearing up the rules of debate and the Speaker, the Honourable Pierre Blondin, forthwith threatened to name him. But Red Michael had the bit in his teeth, not an unusual occurrence.   At social gatherings, provided they were sufficiently social, he was wont to sing "Toreador" with great vigour and feeling, but with his own interpretation of Mr. Bizet's musical conception.   This time he was not singing; but the results were even more serious.   The Speaker uttered the fateful words, "Dr. Clark, I name you."   Sensation!   Anti-climax!   The Sergeant-at-Arms, resplendent, though not formidable; in chain and sword of office, got up from his seat near the door, looked inquiringly and rather helplessly about, and nothing happened.   The roof persistently refused to fall.   Then one of the leaders of the House, Borden himself, if I remember rightly, realizing that something had to be done if the dignity of Parliament was to be preserved—it was wilting rapidly—proceeded to pour oil upon the troubled waters. An apology was made, an empty formality—but it sufficed. I am fairly sure that no member has been named since, and it is highly probable that none ever will.

But while this naming episode was something of a fizzle, the House of Commons upon another occasion had managed to assert its authority, though not over one of its own members. This happened at a time when the Borden Opposition was diligently engaged in prospecting for scandals with the object of discrediting the Laurier Government. Certain transactions in western lands, more especially timber lands, the merits or demerits of the North Atlantic Trading Company, the digging of useless canals and the building of unnecessary wharves, were all live subjects and were debated with extreme ferocity. But perhaps the most succulent of these scandals centred in the administration of the Marine Department and there was an investigation by a judge. At this date I am not clear as to whether the judicial investigation or an inquiry by one of the Commons' committees was responsible for an incident which I believe was without precedent in this country and has never been repeated. A merchant or agent, or something of the kind, who had been doing business with the Marine Department, declined to furnish information demanded of him. Persisting in his refusal, he was summoned to the Bar of the House and there formally questioned. Still obdurate and probably nursing a belief that the Commons could do no more or no worse than administer some sort of reprimand, this gentleman defied the Parliament of Canada. What was to be done with him? One or two members facetiously inclined, or sharing the delinquent's illusion of immunity, advised that he be sent to the Tower. This was impracticable inasmuch as the Tower had nothing in it but an interminable winding staircase. But this time the House was in earnest. It had suffered a deliberate affront. Its dignity had been flouted, and by an outsider. To the everlasting surprise of the man at the Bar, he found himself sentenced to imprisonment and marched off to the Carleton County Gaol, where he remained until the end of the session, at which time the writ of Parliament no longer ran and he was permitted to depart a sadder and, to a limited extent, a wiser man.

. . . . . .

Until the two parties became deadlocked in the naval combat, no Government in this country had ever been in a position to protect itself against organized obstruction. But other Parliaments had found a remedy, and the Borden ministry borrowed it. For the first time the Closure, otherwise known as the "Gag," came into use in Canada. When it was applied, the procedure was simple enough. Mr. Hazen, afterwards Sir Douglas Hazen, moved that "the question be now put." Instantly the House was in an uproar, Opposition members crying "Shame," and charging the Government with cowardice, while Conservative members earnestly besought their opponents to take their medicine. Sir Wilfrid Laurier, who had been brought up standing by the Gag procedure, was furiously angry.

He protested vehemently and fluently, but without avail. The deadlock was broken. On the third reading of the bill, which was not reached until the middle of May, one Liberal amendment after another was voted down. Laurier himself moved the six-months' hoist, the motion many years before had brought to an end the debate on the Manitoba School issue and precipitated the election which sent the Liberal party into office for fifteen years. It failed to stop the Naval Bill, but the Liberal party had still a weapon in reserve—a Senate majority. This majority, headed by Sir George Ross, former Premier of Ontario, sent the measure back to the Commons with an amendment requiring that it be submitted to the country, an amendment which the Government could not, of course, accept.

And in the next year the storm broke. There had been something of an emergency after all.

.   .   .   .   .   .

On June 11, 1583, Sir Humphrey Gilbert sailed out of Plymouth with the *Golden Hind* and four other ships, to found a world. More than three centuries later, a great fleet of giant vessels, carrying the first of Canada's army, sailed into the harbour of Plymouth. Many, many thousands of English people stood upon the cliffs and on the Hoe and watched these long grey ships come in. I think that they were seeing something else. I think the *Golden Hind* came home.

I shall not attempt to deal here with Canada's part in the great conflict of 1914-1918. I do not think the history of the war will ever be written. Attempts have been made, of course, and more will

follow. Volumes of verbiage and statistics have
been, and will be, produced, but they do not, and
will not, tell the story, and for the simple reason that
it cannot be done. The resources of no living
language are adequate to the task of recording the
misery that the war brought upon the world's
people, or to measure the effects of the economic
disturbance for which it was responsible, or to
estimate the injuries inflicted upon civilization.
Consider the fact that millions of men either died
or were ruined physically, and that they were the
flower of the race, the strongest, the fittest, and in
large measure the most high-minded. Who is to
calculate the effect upon the world's future from the
elimination of a posterity which, under normal
conditions of life, those men would have fathered.
Nor is it necessary to go even that far. The war
took out of the world's productive activity the
cream of mankind and kept it out for four years.
As many as thirty million men are said to have
been under arms at one time during those four
years of horror, and probably two-thirds of that
number were destroying instead of producing for
most of that period. It is scarcely surprising that
the world has not recovered from so disastrous an
economic dislocation. The war, moreover, stirred
the pool of humanity to its muddy depths and, as
happens in every such convulsion; there came to the
surface in the subsequent years of peace—if it was
peace—the deadly crawling things whose only fitting
habitat is the darkness and the slime. And they
are with us now, some of them in positions of vast
authority, with a capacity and an inclination for
incalculable mischief.

Woodrow Wilson's avowed object was to make the world safe for democracy. The task of statesmen today, largely by reason of what he did, is to make democracy safe for the world, to save it from itself. Fascism and Nazi-ism are not a satisfying alternative. They take us back to the days before Runnymede, to worse things than any of the Caesars ever attempted, or the Borgias. They cannot survive because they are contrary to the deepest rooted instincts of the race, but they threaten to bring the world down with them into a ruin from which the rebuilding will be a long and indefinitely protracted torture.

Socialism cannot be the answer. It is the negation of individualism and a bar against personal ambition and personal effort and personal success. It excludes everything that has made human progress possible. It is unnatural that any civilization or any theory of social development should originate in the belly rather than in the mind. Civilization is an old dog which may occasionally be taught a new trick or two, but it remains the same dog, responding to the same instincts, even to the same passions, and capable of enrichment only through the applied genius of the individual. The kind of democracy envisaged by Woodrow Wilson was expressed in a formula in which socialists saw or thought they saw their charter, and socialism advanced rapidly under the operation of the Versailles Treaty and the covenant which it embodied. Why was it that British organized labour and its counterpart in this country, which used to preach pacifism and disarmament, became so warlike in 1938? Is not the true answer to be

found in the fact that the democracies were threatened by nations in which socialism, as understood
and practised in Anglo-Saxon countries, and for
that matter in France, cannot exist? Socialism
would have had Democracy to save it from the whip
of the dictator, but who then would have saved
Democracy from Socialism?

Wilson was an idealist, and idealism cannot run
in double harness with the realities of practical
statesmanship. The world knows that now, but is
still paying for the knowledge and will go on paying
in treasure and in blood. The Allies waged a war
that was to end war and, having won it, they
committed the supreme blunder of seeking an
enduring peace in the terms and conditions of a
predatory formula which even a richly gilded frame
of Utopian conception could not redeem.

.   .   .   .   .   .

The declaration of war on the fateful August 4,
1914, was received in no light-hearted spirit by the
Canadian Government. No one could foresee then
that the whole world would be embroiled and that
for four long years, terrible, wearing and exhausting
years, the issue would remain in doubt. Nevertheless, it was a grave and serious business and Ottawa
ministers moved about, heavy with the responsibility
that had come upon them. Yet they moved
swiftly and with a precision that was altogether
admirable. There was, I believe, a mobilization
plan of sorts in the Militia Department, prepared in
advance on the advice of men who had believed
that war was coming, but at the best it could have
been no more than a guide to the performance of the

great task that the formal declaration of hostilities made necessary. There was a great deal said not so long ago as to the circumstances and conditions under which the Canadian people would enter another war.

There were some who went the length of saying that we would have a general election as a means of determining our state of mind, the assumption being, of course, that the enemy would obligingly stand at ease while the campaign was in progress. It is an attractive thought, as these speculative absurdities so often are.

There was no talk of waiting in 1914. The Government could not, as a matter of fact, move fast enough for public opinion. A special session of Parliament was summoned, but only to formalize a course upon which the country had already embarked and upon which there was no division of public sentiment. No sooner was war declared than commanding officers all over the Dominion offered their services. Regiment after regiment volunteered as units. Civilians in all walks of life, in a flood of telegrams to the Government, placed themselves at the disposal of the State. The Militia Department, with a division of something like twenty thousand men in mind, found five times that number clamouring to go. More than thirty thousand assembled in the great camp at Valcartier, and they were only the first. Half a million men were to go out of this country between that time and the end of the war, and sixty thousand of them were destined never to return. "Their name liveth . . . ."

In the 1938 crisis a Canadian Government, to

its eternal discredit, was guilty of the sorriest, the most shameful and humiliating example of political pusillanimity ever known in a British country. While other Dominions and even the native princes of India were openly declaring their loyalty to the Empire and their readiness to support the British Government in the event of war, Canada, at least officially, had nothing to say. And the only explanation was that the British Government had not asked this country for any commitment. Of course it had not, but it cannot have been other than disagreeably surprised to find the Canadian Government waiting for such a request. The miserable truth is that the King Government, with a general election only a little way off, endeavoured to preserve its own popularity with the French-Canadian population as a matter of more concern than the safety of the Empire. And this, unhappily, will always be the case with a government at Ottawa which is not imbued with the British spirit and permits the French-Canadian tail to wag the Anglo-Saxon dog. All Canadian governments, fortunately for this country's self-respect, are not like that. It just happened that we had the wrong kind when the crisis came, a government which, though nominally British, out-Heroded the United States in its attitude of selfish detachment and aloofness. If Britain's prestige suffered by reason of the September sacrifice, Canada was left without any. Contemplating the inactivity of that period there is perhaps all the greater reason to appreciate and acknowledge the prompt action of this same Government in September, 1939.

I am going to give here some correspondence

which passed between Mr. H. A. Gwynne, editor of the London *Morning Post*, and myself in the autumn of 1916. It has to do with the conduct of Sir Sam Hughes as Canada's War Minister, and I am anxious that it should not leave a false impression. I knew Sir Sam for many years as a private member and as a minister, in Opposition and in office. He was a supreme egotist, but he possessed fine qualities and I knew from personal contact and observation that he rendered a service to the Dominion of which, in some important respects, no one of his contemporaries in Canada would have been capable. His energy was enormous. He knew the militia from top to bottom and from end to end. His patriotism and zeal were beyond computation. Moreover, he possessed one virtue that was indispensable in the initial stages of Canada's war effort. Red tape is an army fetish. Had it remained so, the first Canadian division would not have reached the field nearly as early as it did, and we know that its presence in the Ypres salient was a matter of supreme importance to the Allied cause. Sam Hughes cut through formalities, discarded traditional procedure, and turned his broad back upon precedent as if these things had never been. And in the formative period, when organization had to be created and built out of next to nothing, his vigour and his self-given freedom of action were of inestimable value. If he had stopped there and then he would have left a very great name. But as the war continued, the very qualities that had been such valuable assets became more and more productive of trouble, official embarrassment and of general dissatisfaction and discontent. In October of 1914 I received from Mr. Gwynne two letters, one personal, though the subjects were not different, and one for such use as I could make of it. Writing from London under date of October 9, he said:

I have just come back from a visit to the Front and I have had several opportunities of seeing the Canadian rank and file. Their wonderful physique, their splendid courage, and their keenness to beat the Germans, are all qualities which strike one with admiration; but it would be idle and wrong to shut one's eyes to the fact that, in the ranks of the Canadian contingent, there is a considerable amount of dissatisfaction and discontent which will undoubtedly find a very violent outlet when they return home. The chief—indeed, the only—cause of the discontent appears to be a firm conviction on the part of the Canadian soldier that his leaders are appointed by political influence; and they resent this with a deep anger. They say that this is a war in which a mistake made by a leader may cost them their lives; and while they do not mind political "ramps" in peace time they think that, in war time, they are criminal.

I was trying to put the other point of view before some of the many Canadians with whom I talked and I said that, in my opinion, the Canadian Government had gone on the assumption that Canada could manufacture an army quite as well as Great Britain, and the Canadian civilians were just as capable of becoming battalion, brigade, and divisional commanders as were the English. This seemed to arouse their mirth and they pointed out that there was this essential difference; that in England the organization of the new armies was based on the organization of the old army, which was undoubtedly the best in the world. This is confirmed by a conversation which I had the other day with General Balfourier, who commands a French corps and who was fighting on our right recently. He was also one of the defenders of Verdun, and he is a man whose opinion is considered by the French General Staff to be of great weight. He told me quite bluntly that he would give anything to have one hundred of our English soldiers in every one of his battalions; that the British Army organized by Sir Douglas Haig had surpassed the French both in infantry and in artillery tactics; and that although the assembling of such a large army was in itself a miracle, he considered that the greater miracle was the admirable organization which had made it the finest fighting machine in the world.

I can quite see, however, that Canada should endeavour to make the Canadian army as far as possible out of her own material altogether. But in order that this should be successful it is essential that promotions and appointments should be strictly in accordance with merit. In the English Army, for example, there are men who started as sergeants who are now battalion and brigade commanders; but they were appointed purely on their merits as soldiers, and for no other reason. But I am sorry to say that in the Canadian Army politics is playing a most unsavoury part. I hate to say this because I have such an admiration for all that Canada has done and is doing for the Empire and also for the magnificent spirit which she has displayed. Nevertheless, I am unburdening myself to you because I hope that you will be able to point out to the "powers that be" what terrible harm is being done to the Canadian reputation by allowing politics to play a part in military matters.

Some of the English papers have begun to take up what appears on the face of it to be nothing short of a scandal and, although I refuse to join in the campaign, I think that the facts should be brought before you. Surgeon-General Carlton Jones, the Director of the Canadian Medical Service, has been doing extremely good work here; I happen to know this from the War Office here. Now there seems to be a sort of conspiracy to displace him for another medical man who has never had any military training. When I was in Paris recently I saw the Canadian hospital; indeed, even our own people asked me to go and see it in order to see how well the thing is run. To move the D.C.M.S. now would be

nothing short of a hideous blunder and would create
such dissatisfaction among the Canadian rank and file
that, if it does take place, I am really afraid of a violent
outbreak which must affect considerably the party to
which Sir Sam Hughes belongs.   The methods by which
this change is to be effected have caused extreme disgust
throughout the whole of the armed forces of the English
and other Dominions now fighting in France.

On August 19 a divisional order was published on the
instructions of the General Officer Commanding the
Canadian Training Division, appointing a board of
officers to inquire into and report on the administration
of the Canadian Army Medical Corps.   The President
of this board was Colonel H. A. Bruce who, I am told,
has had practically no experience as an army medical
authority.   The appointment of this Court is contrary
to all military precedence.   The only people who could
appoint such a Court would be the Government of
Canada and even then, I imagine, it would appoint a
Court through the R.A.M.C. authorities in London,
under whose orders the Canadian D.M.S. has been
placed.   But for an inquiry to be ordered into the
organization of the Canadian Army Medical Corps by
means of a divisional order was so much opposed to all
military precedent, that it was at once put down as a
political "ramp."   The effect of it was that subordinate
officers of the D.C.M.S. were requested to sit upon a
board of inquiry regarding his methods of administration.
The thing, of course, is so ridiculous that everybody
thinks that it is merely intended to get rid of the D.C.M.S.

But worse followed.   The findings of the Board were
placed in the hands of the D.C.M.S. on September 22.
Two extra copies were given to him on the 24th with
instructions that his answer should be ready and in the
hands of the Minister at 12 noon on the 27th.   It was
absurd to expect that any proper answer could be given
in such a short space of time.   The report is unsigned,
and for the obvious reason that the signatures would
show that it was a Board of subordinate officers asked to
report on the office of their Chief.   If the Canadian

Government were under the impression that the Canadian D.M.S. was not carrying out his duties properly, it would have been their right to send out a commission to inquire into the matter; but I have no hesitation in saying that the present move is nothing less than an attempt to get rid of the D.C.M.S. in order to place in his stead a personal friend of the War Minister. If this is done there will be a disaster; for the Canadian soldiers are so proud of the admirable way in which they are looked after in their hospitals, that this tampering with their most sensitive point will produce an acute form of discontent which will be bound to make itself heard.

It is only to avoid this that I write to you this letter.

To this and the accompanying letter I replied on November 7 as follows:

Your two letters of October 9 reached me on the 23rd, in time, I think, to be of good service in bringing things to a head. Sir Thomas White had already left Ottawa but I showed the longer letter to Sir Robert Borden. He seemed very much impressed by it and at his request I left a copy with him, without the identification marks. He informed me then that steps would be taken to remedy the conditions, or some of them, described by you. Since then the announcement of Sir George Perley's appointment as Minister of the Overseas Forces, has been made. It is a long step toward the elimination of Sir Sam Hughes, the weight of whose mistakes had become over heavy for the Government. Sir Sam is now in the country, ostensibly on a hunting expedition, and the Department here is under the direction of Mr. F. B. McCurdy, Parliamentary Secretary, a very safe man. The situation now is that Sir Sam Hughes is still nominally Minister of Militia, but that practically all the more important branches of the military administration have been detached and placed under the control of other men. It was easier to remove the office than to remove the Minister.

A copy of the body of your letter to me has been sent

to Sir George Perley by the Prime Minister, attached to a covering letter which I have seen. I think you can rest assured that a great many of the abuses will be corrected, and that the threatened displacement of Surgeon-General Carlton Jones will not take place.

It is not understood here that politics have influenced the appointment of officers in the overseas army. I mean that there has been no great preference shown for Conservatives because they are Conservatives. What actually has happened is just as bad or worse, certainly worse from the standpoint of party peace. The appointments have been made by Sir Sam Hughes either to please his friends or to enrage his enemies. It has been a matter of personal, rather than of political, influence. As a matter of fact there has been a strong conviction in the minds of Conservative members that Sir Sam Hughes has been showing far too much consideration to the Liberals. This has been one of Sir Robert Borden's troubles. Furious protests have been made to him, members have threatened to resign and the party generally has been in a more or less constant state of unrest bordering upon revolt. I could give you quite an imposing list of prominent Liberals who have been given important military commands by Sir Sam Hughes. The Government, and the party either for that matter, have not objected to the appointment of Liberals who are qualified and who happen to be the best men available, but Sir Sam Hughes has shown a disposition to go out of his way in order to strengthen himself with the other side and to secure partial immunity from criticism. In the latter, he has failed.

The whole situation here, so far as the military administration is concerned, has been very unpleasant. There will be an improvement from now on. Sir Sam Hughes has been shorn of most, if not all, of his power to do harm, and Sir George Perley has instructions to straighten things out overseas.

Surgeon-General Carlton Jones was superceded, but subsequently re-instated. I should like to say here that the part played by Colonel H. A. Bruce should not be considered as coming within the scope of the criticism which was levelled against the minister. Colonel Bruce's reputation stands too high in this country to permit any possible misconstruction of either his motives or his conduct. He was an officer acting under orders and he discharged the duty to which he was assigned.[1] His later career has been one of exceptional distinction.

Sir Sam Hughes left the ministry in November, 1916. He had resigned. It is probably true that he had served his own vanity and that of his friends and that his time as minister had been one of keen enjoyment and great personal glory. Nevertheless, he had not spared himself either physically or mentally, nor had he spared others, and he had achieved much. If he had imagined himself wearing the imperial purple of the Caesars, his dream had been a very active one and it is my personal feeling that what he actually accomplished ought to have a larger place in the public memory than the blunders of favouritism which set him at odds with his colleagues and brought about his official downfall.

No one will seek in these pages a record of the troubles that beset the Government in this mid-war period. Those who are scavenger-minded may go if they like to the official archives for the facts disclosed in the inquiry into the work of the original Shell Commission which preceded the Imperial Munitions Board, and the most that they will find is

1Details of the controversy of 1916 regarding the Canadian Military Establishment in England may be found in Sir Andrew McPhail's *History of the Canadian Forces, 1914-1919—The Medical Services*, Chap. VIII.
Sir Sam Hughes died August 24, 1921.

that the Commission under Sir Alexander Bertram did what the majority of people had believed to be impossible, organized the mobilization of Canadian industry and its rapid adaptation to the business of shell production on an enormous scale. They will find that the Imperial Munitions Board had a broad foundation upon which to build. They may perhaps ascertain something more to their liking, assuming that they are upon the lookout for unpleasantness, in the investigation conducted by a parliamentary committee into the manufacture of army boots. Even there, however, they will discover nothing comparable to the classic episode of the Crimea, where somebody acted under the impression that an army walked on one foot only. The Committee did obtain a more or less liberal education on the subject of side leathers, split leather, etc., and the relative merits of tanning sole leather by the oak and hemlock processes. Also the investigation was an excellent thing for a number of lawyers. The whole business was very soon forgotten in the rush of more important events and the pressure of more formidable problems.

Toward the end of 1916, the Government was seriously perplexed by discouraging results in the various recruiting areas, not excluding the Province of Quebec, and compulsory service became a subject of open discussion. No one liked the word "conscription," and the Government was strongly disinclined to take what was becoming an inevitable step. But the situation in France was critical. Canada was aiming at an army of half a million men, and it was becoming evident that the goal could not be reached through voluntary enlistment.

At the same time the reaction of Quebec to conscription could quite easily be foreseen. About this time a masquerade dance was held by a well-known club in western Quebec and some malignant person invented a story that the first prize had been taken by a young French-Canadian of military age disguised as a soldier. It was, of course, an invention, but it did illustrate, and accurately, a feeling then very generally prevalent.

About this time, or a little later, the Government in a final effort to stimulate enlistment without recourse to conscription, established a National Service Board, the purpose of which was to mobilize all the resources of the country, including all the man-power and all the woman-power for the promotion of all kinds of war service. In order to give the maximum effect to this movement, the Prime Minister undertook a rapid tour of the Dominion and R. B. Bennett, M.P., went with him. The Toronto *Mail and Empire* sent me along, and thereby hangs a somewhat alcoholic tale.

Western Canada was dry, not so much for lack of rain but through prohibition and the low standard of efficiency attained by the bootlegging profession on the prairie. A fellow journalist, who had arranged to go with me, conceived it to be our duty to our fellow citizens in the West to take with us an adequate supply of liquid refreshment. It was to be another example of Eastern solicitude for the welfare and comfort of the Western producer, and more particularly in this instance, the Western consumer. We were to travel in the old *Ottawa*, a car belonging to the Department of Railways, and as the party was getting under way in Montreal,

spectators at the Place Viger Station witnessed a
heavy movement of bottled liquors of one kind and
another into this ancient but comfortable vehicle.
At the last minute, and with all this promise of
Western irrigation on board, my fellow benefactor
backed out, leaving me high but by no means dry.
The first National Service meetings were in Montreal
and Quebec and were frequently interrupted by
young hoodlums, despite the gravity of the appeals
made to them by Sir Robert Borden and by leaders
of their own race. Sir Wilfrid Laurier had been
invited to co-operate in the National Service
Movement and had found reasons for declining.
From Quebec the train went west over that costly
folly originally built as the National Transcontinental and the party was afforded an excellent
view of the wilderness through which the line ran,
an experience which did little to remove an earlier
impression as to the monstrous stupidity of the
enterprise. I went into Sir Robert's car one night
for the purpose of informing him that in the event
of his desiring to restore his flagging energies there
were certain cordials to be had in the press car.
"No," he said, "No. I don't think I want anything tonight." I said good-night to him and
turned to the door. He was a cautious man and
accustomed to the revision of his judgments. "By
the way," he said, "what cordials have you?"

There was a large and enthusiastic meeting in
Winnipeg, after which the train headed west to
Saskatoon. A distinguished Western journalist
boarded the train at Winnipeg and I found him in
the morning looking so much the worse for wear that
I was moved to spirituous compassion. He, of

course, knew nothing of my resources. He was an exceedingly miserable man, resembling nothing that even the least discriminating cat would have brought in. "Bill," said I—I am using the name Bill out of delicacy and to conceal his identity. His real name was Fred. "Bill, what you really need is a nice, long, cold John Collins, one in which the soda sizzles and the ice clinks." He gave me an evil look. "Bill," I repeated, "there is nothing like a nice long Collins on a morning like this when you are suffering from overwork." He looked at me again and with a concentrated hatred similar to that with which the victim of a mediæval torture would have regarded an official manipulator of the thumb-screw, the rack, the sheriff's daughter, or some other of the uncomfortable devices and contrivances employed as question-marks by our forthright ancestors. I rang the bell and the steward appeared. "Cecil," said I, "Mr. Limsey would like a John Collins. Make it very long and very cold and put plenty of John in it." "Yes, sir," said the steward and retired. The sufferer went on suffering. He didn't believe it and his head ached with increased intensity. And then the remedy was heard approaching. It burst upon his vision. He gazed incredulously upon it, and then fell upon it. He was as a brand snatched from the burning, a soul renewed, and in his recovery at least the National Service Movement was a success. It was successful also at nearly all the stations along the line and for the same reason. Word of this travelling oasis preceded its movement across the desert and at every stop the car was invaded by delegations of hitherto-unknown friends, moved by a common aridity, who fell upon our necks and upon those of all the bottles that a prudent steward thought fit to produce.

These social amenities, while not constituting the main purpose of the tour, were to a large extent its most satisfactory feature. There were, of course, enthusiastic meetings at which the Prime. Minister's serious presentation of the grave issues involved, and the eloquent exhortations of Mr. Bennett, moved large audiences to high pitches of patriotic fervour. Sir Robert would explain that the Empire had not entered the war for purposes of territorial aggrandizement but for the vindication of a great principle, after which one of the leading choirs or choral societies of the community would rise and sing "Wider still and wider shall thy bounds be set. God that made thee mighty, make thee mightier yet." After which we would all go home feeling greatly uplifted.

The tour took us to Edmonton, Vancouver and Victoria and back via various prairie cities which had not been touched on the westward journey. It was December and very, very cold. I know of one journalist who refused to leave the train at Brandon after once putting his nose outside the door of the car. The Prime Minister, upon returning in a condition of acute discomfort by reason of a temperature of forty below or thereabouts, referred in terms of considerable bitterness to this journalist's rigid observance of nature's first law. It was abundantly evident that upon that occasion at least Sir Robert would rather have been a newspaperman than Prime Minister. The tour ended in Toronto, with the fine meetings which that city always provides, but so far as recruiting was concerned, the whole business was a failure. In the following year Canada knew that conscription had to come, and it came.

· · · · · ·

The miserable truth about the whole situation in regard to French-Canadian enlistments is that the situation was mishandled from the first. I believe I am safe in saying that immediately after the declaration of war, two eminent French-Canadians were prepared to raise a Quebec battalion for service in France, and submitted their offer to the Minister of Militia. They stipulated, and naturally, that this battalion should be officered by French-Canadians, particularly in order to maintain its racial complexion but partly also for the very practical reason that officers and men should speak a mutually understandable language. General Hughes refused and a great deal of damage was done. Some of it was repaired when the second division was being organized, but I believe the initial affront was never wholly forgotten or forgiven. Another blunder consisted in the selection of recruiting officers who appeared to be chosen on the basis of their maximum unfitness to deal with French-Canadians whether from a racial or religious point of view. For example, a Methodist minister from somewhere in Ontario would not make the strongest possible appeal to French-Canadian Roman Catholic youth, yet the Department, if not the minister, appointed one of these worthy gentlemen to attempt that very thing. Under more enlightened direction much, if not all, of the Quebec trouble could have been avoided, and probably would have been. A great many French-Canadians did serve in the war, as officers and privates, and they acquitted themselves as well there as did the bravest and most loyal of the men from other provinces or from other countries.

.   .   .   .   .   .

On February 3, 1916, the old Parliament Building was destroyed by fire. The House had commenced its evening sitting and was engaged, without personal bias, in a spirited discussion of lobsters. I was not present at the time as these debates on the manners and customs of Nova Scotian crustacea by members who quite evidently had come from the same neighbourhood always perplexed me with doubts as to the true origin of Maritime politicians. For that and other reasons I was elsewhere. As a matter of fact, I narrowly escaped the dubious distinction of being cremated in that part of the building devoted to the liquid stage of after-dinner discussions. It was a large room, though on a good thirsty night I have seen it filled to capacity. On this memorable occasion there were only two occupants. That excellent journalist, raconteur, bon-vivant and astute politician, the late Tom Blacklock, one of the best-known and best-liked newspapermen of his generation, was one of them. He and I were considering important public issues, the precise nature of which I do not now recall. Nor am I clear whether we had exhausted the subject or whether there remained an argument or two at the bottom of the bottle. The point is that we had to leave and leave hurriedly. We were, I believe, the last people to go down that elevator.

When we reached the main floor, the place was in a turmoil. Smoke was pouring through the corridors, shadowy figures were appearing and disappearing, members were scrambling out of the Commons' Chamber in inky, smoky darkness, the lights having gone out. Dr. Clark was crying hysterically that men had been left behind, a mistake, fortunately, although Bowman B. Law, Liberal member for Yarmouth, N.S., did not answer to the subsequent roll call and nothing that could be identified as part of him was ever found. The belief was that he died in some other part of the building. John Baptiste LaPlante, Assistant Clerk of the House, a very quiet, very efficient little man, died in his upstairs office. They found him near the window. In all, seven persons lost their lives, including two women, guests, who were trapped in the Speaker's Chambers.

The newspapermen, having got out of the front door—at least I did—bethought them of their immediate responsibilities. Having escaped the fire, it was their business to inform the outside world of what was happening. We got into the press room by means of a ladder and an open window, groped around in the smoke and rescued what we could. I took my old typewriter, carried it down to the office of the Ottawa *Citizen* and worked from there. I still have that old typewriter, though it reposes in honourable retirement. I have had it for thirty-three years, and it has produced, I suppose, a good many miles of newspaper copy.

The fire started in the reading-room and could

not have chosen a better place.   There was old, dry woodwork everywhere, with a lot of varnish on it. Even the stands for the newspapers were of wood. From this super-efficient firebox a short corridor led round to the Commons' Chamber and the fire roared through it.   The whole of the Commons' wing was soon in flames from cellar to roof and the windows were belching fire.   The Senate wing seemed secure, but prudent folk took down from the walls the enormous gilt-framed portraits of dead and gone statesmen and a fine picture of Queen Victoria, which hung in the Senate hall, and carted them out into the snow.   The Senate, I am inclined to think, was not in session that night.   It seldom was, or is.   There was time enough, however, for the elder statesmen to have left the building before the fire got into that wing, and it did get there. There was no stopping it.   The whole building had been cleverly adapted to destruction by this formidable element and it was not long before the entire block, with all its historical associations, was blazing to the sky.   Up the great Central Tower went the flames.   I have seen many conflagrations, great and small; I have seen half a city burning and its inhabitants camping in the fields, but I have never witnessed anything to equal or nearly equal the spectacle, at once awful and magnificent, of that flaming tower.   It sent a solid pillar of twisting, billowing gold up into the winter night.   It was stupendous and unforgettable.

When the ruins cooled, people picked up here and there shapeless bits of metal and of glass that had once been the household effects of the Parliament of Canada.

The suggestion that this fire had been of incendiary origin, the nefarious work of German agents, was natural under the conditions then prevailing. The Great War had been raging for a year and a half, and the public mind was full of suspicion. Indeed the idea was taken so seriously that the Government ordered a thorough investigation for the purpose of determining the true origin of the catastrophe and of settling, once and for all, the rumours that were flying about. The inquiry was exhaustive, but unproductive, and no one knows to this day whether the destruction of this famous building, with its attendant loss of life, was the deliberate act of an enemy alien or was caused, as many believed at the time, by the careless handling of a cigarette by some member or official of the House while reading his hometown newspaper. The real marvel is that the place had not been burned long before.

The question of rebuilding was taken up immediately and the first thought was to make use of the remaining walls, which had been tested, and to erect upon them a legislative building which would be, in exterior form at least, a replica of the old. Unfortunately—to my mind, at any rate—this sensible plan was abandoned and the Government proceeded to spend from twelve to fourteen million dollars of the country's money, much of it needlessly. Parliament moved, perhaps instinctively, to the Museum.

The Victoria Memorial Museum had been erected some few years before on McLeod Street, facing up Metcalfe Street toward Parliament Hill. It was hurriedly refitted for the reception and accommodation of a homeless legislature, the tem-

porary Senate chamber being separated from the
permanent fossil exhibit by a wooden partition.
The Commons went to the other end of the building,
still observing the ancient theory that the right
hand of Parliament does not know what the left
hand is doing.   In the Commons, be it known, you
are not permitted to refer directly to the Upper
House.   The extreme limit of parliamentary detachment and reserve is reached in an oblique allusion
to something that has happened "in another place."
The Senate is among the untouchables; it has not
even a name.

There is a story about this Museum. In the
days of its adolescence it had a tower, a large square
thing of stone with an ornamental top.   Unhappily,
its foundations had been laid in shifting soil.   The
Government which had built it had been warned by,
I think, the contractor, certainly by others connected
with the work of construction, that the tower
footings were all wrong and that at some time or
other the whole kaboodle would come down.   These
warnings were unheeded; the tower was built and it
did appear to have the solidity of the everlasting
hills.   Its feet, however, were of clay, and the clay
moved.   The tower manifested a dislike for the rest
of the building and began to edge away from it.
The nomadic proclivities of this majestic but
wayward edifice aroused official alarm.   It was
feared that some of the ornamental stonework
surmounting the tower might detach itself without
notice and fall to earth, possibly glancing off the
cerebrum of a passing parliamentarian—and these
stones were valuable.   It became necessary to
anticipate the obvious intentions of the tower and

take it down. That is why it is not there now. However, the Museum served very well as a substitute for the lamented Houses of Parliament and there for some considerable time, when debates were not in progress, the laws of the land were made. It was during that period of wandering in the wilderness that I left the Press Gallery, which had been my home for fourteen years. My colleagues sent me off with a handsome cigar case of silver and gold, and with their blessing. We made little speeches and a cabinet minister or two joined in these affectionate farewells. I moved to greater responsibilities, but away from the joy of battle.

9

Suns and Satellites

NATURALLY, in my early
newspaper training, I had seen a great many people
sent behind the bars, miserable offscourings of the
street, both sexes included, and offenders of every
intervening class up to that of murderer. I have
seen bank managers, fresh from richly furnished
offices, standing in the dock *en route* to the peniten-
tiary, usually because circumstances had been too
much for them. I have been in prisons and gaols
myself on numerous occasions, though only in a
business capacity, but on one occasion which I
remember to my everlasting contrition, I was the
means of sending a fellow craftsman to the lock-up;
and we were hundreds of miles apart.

It happened that in 1916, or thereabouts, a Royal
Commission under the presidency of a very Liberal

judge was investigating some major errors of judgment on the part of the Roblin (Conservative) Government in Manitoba. In some way or other the Commission had fallen foul of a section of the provincial press and had assumed a rather dictatorial attitude toward newspapers and newspaper criticism.

The Honourable Robert Rogers, who had been a Roblin minister, was then a member of the Borden cabinet in Ottawa as Minister of Public Works. He was looked upon as the bad boy of both administrations, the practical politician, one or more of whom is to be found in every government. Even the peerless Mowat had his "wicked partner" in Ontario. Laurier himself had one or two and was wont to close his eyes and ears to their more reprehensible doings and the rumours thereof. But Bob Rogers had redeeming virtues; he was friendly, generous, intensely loyal to his party, and he was not a quitter. He had no love for this Manitoba investigation or for the principal investigator, which was scarcely surprising.

When the press incident arose in Manitoba he and the late Senator William Dennis of Halifax put their heads together and conceived a plot. They came to me and suggested that Tom Blacklock and I should prepare an article in vigorous support of newspaper freedom, which article Senator Dennis would then publish in his newspaper, the Halifax *Herald*, whence it, or the substance of it, would be telegraphed to Winnipeg. Blacklock and I agreed with the utmost enthusiasm, but Tom, with the presence of mind that was characteristic of him, left the actual perpetration of the crime to me. I took a very lofty stand. A free press and a free people were synonymous and indivisible, and so forth. Rogers and Dennis were in high spirits. The screed went to Halifax, appeared prominently in the Halifax *Herald*, and was sent to Winnipeg as the *Herald's* product. Most of the Winnipeg editors, I think, fought shy of it, but some, casting discretion to the winds, made use of it, and the Commission very promptly sent them to gaol. Their incarceration was not, I am glad to say, a lengthy one, and one or two of them still walk the earth in all health and in excellent spirits. They did not know that they were punished for a crime that I committed, but they wouldn't have cared if they had.

.   .   .   .   .   .

One does not follow elections in Canada without finding himself, at some time or other, on the edge of the mud. Not that electoral corruption is any more prevalent in this country than in others. I have formed the impression that it is epidemic and that, on the whole, Canadian politics are free from its worst phases. In these I do not include the practice, sanctified by time and custom, of wholesale bribery of the people through preferential expenditures of their own money, or the promises of similar expenditures which are made by an Opposition party always indifferent to the possibility of having to meet its political I.O.U.'s. Parliament in the early part of the 1938 session, greeted with unctuous approval—and subsequently shelved—a Government measure designed to cleanse electoral campaigns of any and all improprieties, more especially in the collection and use of party funds— the war chests, the things to which the late J. Israel

Tarte alluded in his memorable understatement that elections are not won through prayerful exercises. It seems to me that there is much less need now for such legislation than there was a quarter of a century ago, or perhaps a little before that, when, in the Province of Ontario especially, corruption was rampant and those who practised it were unashamed.

The most extraordinary incident that I recall in this regard is a conspiracy to steal the West Hastings election, in 1904, by means of trick ballot boxes. These boxes, which were imported from the United States, were fitted with secret compartments into which the Conservative votes were to go, a more or less equal number of bogus ballots being marked for the Liberal candidate and deposited in the box proper. It was an ingenious idea, but those responsible for it came to grief. The intention to use the boxes in East Hastings was not carried out, but in the west riding they made their appearance in some if not all of the polling booths. The trouble was that one of the conspirators told the Conservative candidate and, as luck would have it, rumour began to associate this innocent victim with the enterprise which was intended for his undoing. He very properly brought an action for criminal libel, which, I think, succeeded, at least to the extent of a committal for trial, but the libel caused no such stir as the evidence in regard to the conspiracy itself. A number of arrests were made and one of the individuals implicated left the country. Apart from this departure, and so far as my memory goes, the consequences to the individuals concerned were not very severe, but the trial was a *cause célèbre* and its developments were followed with the keenest possible interest throughout Canada and only to a lesser extent in the United States and Great Britain. The old city of Belleville had, in this episode, one of its biggest moments, I think the last of them, and it was a long time ago.

At a later date, and in this same area, there was another election trial. The return of either a Liberal or Conservative, I forget which, was protested, and the trial began in all solemnity and ceremony. After the opening proceedings it seemed likely that the protest would succeed. The court adjourned and some time thereafter I was in my hotel room engaged in friendly converse with one or two competing scribes when voices drifted in through a door communicating with the adjoining room. Please believe that we were not eavesdropping. What we heard was unavoidable. It was the plaintive protest of an eminent member of the Ontario Bar, a man of high reputation and unsullied integrity, who was being called upon to make what would be, in a maiden, the first false step. "I have never," he was saying, "done anything like this before." With this pathetic appeal to a blameless past, the protesting Donna Julia consented on behalf of his party to a saw-off.

The practice used to be more common than it is now. One party protests the election of the other party's candidate. The other party, thereupon, unless it has a protest of its own already in hand, looks around for an opposing member-elect who has managed to edge in with a narrow and probably insecure majority. Then the parties get together and one says, "You drop your protest and we'll

drop ours." It is economical and seems fair, but in
actual operation the saw-off is not unlike poker,
and the benefit goes to the best bluffer. In the
incident that I have mentioned, the worst harm done
was to the conscience of a counsel previously proud
of his probity.

        .   .   .   .   .   .

At more or less regular intervals people ask me
how the parliaments of these days compare with
those of pre-war times. It is a question not easily
answered for the reason that the onlooker's standards themselves undergo a process of readjustment
as the years pass, that his personal relationships
alter, and, to some extent, his judgment. Nevertheless it is my opinion, as it is, I know, of others, that
the federal parliament has degenerated and that the
same is true in greater or less degree of provincial
legislatures. If these various parliamentary bodies
reflect accurately and precisely the average culture,
spirit and ethical conception of the nation as a
whole—and they should do better than that—it
seems to follow that a very general retrogression has
taken place. This is not an agreeable conclusion
and I hesitate to accept it, but I do still believe
that, man for man, the parliaments of today are
distinctly and seriously inferior to their predecessors.
They may be endowed with a much greater legislative fecundity, but that is not necessarily desirable.
A certain procreative exuberance is, I believe,
characteristic of the rodentia. Legislation, whether
of a public or private character, cannot properly be
measured in terms of quantity or volume. Quality
must be the first consideration of all, and the quality

of our laws is dependent upon the collective ability of those who make them.

It may be true that a comparatively young man, seeing a Dominion parliament for the first time, may find himself impressed unduly, not only by an environment of creative power but by an atmosphere of authority, and he may fall into the error of accepting statesmanship at its face value, always a dangerous thing to do. I have tried to rid my mind of its earlier impressions, but their removal has not weakened my conviction that the country entrusted its business to better men twenty-five to thirty-five years ago than it is doing now. Of course, it is necessary to make exceptions. There are still men of undoubted ability, integrity and vision in the House of Commons of Canada, and there were men who had narrowly escaped the category of congenital idiocy in the House which I first saw. But the average was higher then than now; of that I am confident. In the earlier period there were more men of outstanding ability in the House of Commons than can be found there today, or than it has been possible to find there for some considerable time. Laurier had the makings of three or four cabinets among his followers, and all of them would have been good. No such condition obtains at Ottawa now or has obtained for many years. The Opposition led by Sir Robert Borden, particularly after the elections of 1904 and 1908, was exceptional in its high aggregate of ability. Upon no basis of comparison can the present Conservative Opposition be likened to it. Where do we find a Macdonald, a Laurier, or even a Sifton nowadays? And if Mr. Bennett suffered in contrast with Sir Robert Borden,

the intellectual disparity between his elected supporters and the men by whom Borden was
surrounded was far more marked. If we go into the
provincial fields we find much the same thing. We
do not attempt to compare a Mitchell Hepburn with
an Oliver Mowat, or a William Aberhart with—
whatever the circumstances of his eclipse—a
Brownlee, and we use much the same discretion in
regard to others.

Sir Lomer Gouin, during the long political career
in his native province and a briefer one at Ottawa,
held the confidence and the respect if not the
affection of his French-Canadian compatriots in an
extraordinary degree, the more extraordinary by
reason of the fact that he lacked the temperamental
characteristics of his compatriots. He had none of
the volatility, none even of the vivacity which
differentiates the Quebec politician from his fellows
in other provinces. The best clue that I can give to
Sir Lomer's mentality may be expressed in the
statement that he thought in English and, by the
same token, many of his closest associates and
friends were English. I do not suggest for one
moment that he stood apart from his race. Rather
he stood up from it, an exceptional product of it,
always a great lover of his province but never
subject to the restraints of provincialism. I saw
him first many years ago when as Attorney-General
of Quebec he addressed the Union of Canadian
Municipalities. Already a man of established reputation, he impressed the members of that Union
with his strong grasp of municipal matters and the
liberality of his treatment of them. The same deep
understanding was manifest in later years in his

discussions of national and international affairs, in his executive sagacity, the sureness of his hand. He could as easily have been a Conservative as a Liberal, not that he was ever anything but a tower of strength to his party, but he was one of the few men of his time who could and would and did put his principles first. He believed in immigration, believed in the tariff, and made no bones about it. He did a great deal to develop the resources and industries of Quebec and he was gaining new prestige and influence as federal Minister of Justice when ill-health overtook him. He passed into history as the ablest of Quebec premiers, one of the few who in the last fifty years could qualify for the rank of statesman and occupy that rank with distinction.

The man who followed him in office at Quebec, Louis Alexandre Taschereau, under whom the long Liberal régime came to an end, was the victim of political longevity. His party had been in office for twenty-three years when he formed his Government. It was to be in office for another fifteen years, but the Government was going to seed. Taschereau himself belonged to a provincial aristocracy and had behind him a great family tradition. His followers, some of them, and members of his administrative staff, some of them, had come to regard themselves as having some political hereditary right in the province and to its resources. In time this sort of thing becomes talked about. If Premier Taschereau could not stop the graft, he could not stop the publicity which, by the year 1935, had brought the party into the gravest disrepute, and, thereafter, he was waging a losing fight. True, he emerged from the final debacle with his own skirts clean, but the mud had come very close to him, close enough to affect a family pride that theretofore had been unbending, and the lustre of a great name.

There is not much pleasure in reflecting upon this downward trend in public life and public service. I am fully aware that in speaking of service I may be confronted with some of the more egregious legislative and administrative errors into which the ninth, tenth and eleventh Parliaments were led, or the blunders of one or two of their immediate successors. But the mistakes then made were committed, on the whole, in good faith—and in the deceptive light of abounding prosperity. Later Parliaments have had the unhappy results of these errors before them. They have had the opportunity and it has been their duty to undo the damage, as far as possible, and they have lacked the necessary visceral valour. Theirs, to my mind, is the greater culpability. But let that pass. The point I should like to make is that if the calibre of men in public office has depreciated, the fault is not theirs so much as it is the fault of the public in its attitude toward its chosen trustees during at least the last two decades. It has been the custom to consider a public servant as a private grafter, to impute the worst rather than the best motives always and in all circumstances, to vilify and traduce, to couple responsibility with distrust and service with suspicion. The public has chosen to think that because there has been a black sheep here and there the whole flock must be condemned, and condemnation has followed. Nothing could be more stupid, nothing less fair. Even men like the Honourable Robert Rogers were not seeking personal enrichment.

Bob Rogers was, of course, one of the bad boys of Canadian politics, a practical politician in the business sense of the term, a manipulator of party funds and party patronage. If this was not generally known, it was generally taken for granted. Rogers himself never appeared to take thought of his reputation, but went serenely on his way doing the things that somebody in every political party has had to do, doing them perhaps a little more brazenly but none the less efficiently. His chickens had come home to roost in Manitoba, and they had been very tough birds. Rogers had left them and moved to a larger sphere of influence.

He was a curious product, a native of Quebec, a sometime storekeeper, but for many years a politician and political fixer. He could not have been a success as a party sheepdog had he not been endowed with some skill and some attractive personal qualities. These things he had, and the fact that he was "Bob" Rogers to every one, friend and foe alike, throws a revealing light on his personality. He was the friend of any man who would accept his friendship. He was generous, and as a party man he was the essence of loyalty. He never pretended to be great, never, so far as I know, pretended to be good, and I knew him quite well. He was a poor speaker, but willing to fill the breach at any time, and if his forehead was low he had quite a considerable area behind the ears, adorned in the tonsorial style set by Sir Wilfrid Laurier. Nothing very good has ever been said about Bob Rogers, but, unlike at least one other whose career paralleled his at a number of important points, he died a poor man. If he had feathered some nests, he had neglected his own.

Any one at all familiar with public men and public affairs in the last thirty-five years can vouch for the statement that the great majority of this country's elected servants, those I mean who have borne the heavy burdens of administration whether at Ottawa or in the provincial capitals, have died impoverished, or have gone out of office relatively poor. Most of these men had given the best of their lives to the State. The passing glory which may have been theirs through political preferment was bought at a heavy price in more or less constant and anxious labour, in the discharge of onerous and delicate responsibilities and, as often as not, in the sacrifice of friendships for the preservation of principle. The State has owed these men immeasurably more than it ever gave them, and the debt can never be repaid; but at least some respect might be paid to their memory and some consideration might be shown for those who have taken their places and are serving to the best of their ability, or, at all events, to the limits of their courage. To group them all as mere "politicians" and smear them with all the sinister implications of a misunderstood and misused term, will never be an effective means of lifting the standard of public life, of inducing abler and bolder men to seek election and accept public administrative responsibility. It is still true that the public gets what it asks for, and it always will be true. Parliaments may reframe election laws and restrict election activities till old age overtakes them, but they will never, by those means alone rectify the two fundamental weaknesses in our political system. One of these is a senseless extravagance in the bestowal of the franchise and the other is the one I have already mentioned, the curious disposition of the people to foul their own nests by everlastingly maligning the men in whose hands they have placed their business.

.   .   .   .   .   .

The general elections of 1896 and 1911, like that of 1878, were fought on great national issues, but as a general rule governments in this country simply wear themselves out. In some instances it takes a very long time, as in the case of the Murray régime in Nova Scotia and the extraordinary Liberal record of Marchand, Parent, Gouin and Taschereau in Quebec. Indeed, the inclination of Canadian electors is to leave well alone, which is reasonable enough, but tolerance sometimes develops into indifference and negligence, and there have been occasions when this has done infinite harm to the country. It is quite apparent now, for example, that the Laurier Government should have been defeated in the election of 1904, before the Grand Trunk Pacific-National Transcontinental monstrosity had gone beyond the paper and discussion stage. Unfortunately, the somewhat limited reasoning power of the Canadian voter was functioning imperfectly at that time. The dinner pail was fairly full and the grandiloquent nonsense uttered by Liberal speakers as a substitute for argument in supporting the Laurier railway programme exerted a kind of hypnotic influence. Much the same sort of thing at a much more recent date induced the people of Alberta to endorse the egregious folly of Social Credit.

And this brings me to one of my favourite obsessions, namely, the looseness of the franchise. It should be unnecessary to refresh ourselves in the knowledge that this franchise was very dearly bought by successive generations of our forebears. If the blood of the martyrs is the seed of the church, it is equally the radical source of our political institutions, though the martyrs were of another class. That being so, the franchise should have some value, should rank as a privilege of citizenship rather than as a right exercisable by people, men, women and children, who know nothing about citizenship. The vote is given indiscriminately and has become a count of heads without regard to the rather important question as to whether the heads have anything in them beyond an assortment of natural lusts. A young man or a young woman of twenty-one years is not a qualified elector, the law to the contrary notwithstanding. The same law permits any number of irresponsible illiterates to nullify the votes of an equal number of the most highly qualified students or masters of political economy or an equal number of men and women having large stakes in the country, and having, therefore, a direct concern in the character of its government. The law permits a criminal to vote upon an equality with a bishop unless he, that is to say the criminal, happens to be in durance vile when the voters' list is being compiled. The same law withholds the franchise from an Indian ordinarily resident on a reservation who may be better qualified than an Indian residing somewhere else, and it assumes that any Indian has achieved intellectual competence through having served in the World War. It is all very confusing. Surely it is something of a miracle that under such conditions worse things have not happened even than the many ghastly legislative blunders that have been committed in the last thirty or forty years. We give the vote to the idler and the wastrel, to any idiot who is not actually confined in an asylum, and, under certain easy conditions, to newcomers in the country, people who have not had the time, if they had the wit, to master the elementary features of our governmental system, men and women with no better background than generations of peasant ignorance—and we expect them to use the franchise intelligently. It may be good democracy but it is not good common sense, and it accounts for the fact that we send to our parliaments at almost every election a group of representatives of whom a major proportion are affiliated with cerebral obesity. It is admittedly difficult to draw the line between the sheep who should vote and the goats who should not. At present these categories are hopelessly mixed and it does seem to me that some standard should be established, possibly a simple standard of education, for observance in the preparation of voters' lists. The present haphazard system cannot possibly make for an expression of informed public opinion and it is wholly inconsistent with the history and value of the franchise. The matter affects me much as the late Mr. Dick was affected by King Charles' head, and it is unnecessary to remind me that Mr. Dick was slightly peculiar.

The worst enemy of any government is, of

course, business depression, and loyal, even competent, service counts for nothing with a populace imbued with the mistaken theory that a government can replace bad times with prosperity overnight. Post-war history is replete with examples of governments in this and other countries which have been turned out of office for no reason at all other than the popular illusion that something different is necessarily something better. The second most dangerous condition arises from the discovery of official corruption, particularly in small things. It is seldom if ever a major steal that arouses the public conscience. More often it is something trifling, at least in terms of money, and the reason for this is that the larger financial coups are beyond the grasp of the average elector. Make him acquainted with some official skullduggery in the purchase of coal oil and he will "throw the grafters out." Something very much like this actually happened many years ago in Quebec, and the moral is that an administration which desires to peculate in safety should do it in a big way. The greater the swag the greater the immunity. Of course, there are times when this sort of thing goes on too long and the aroma, coupled with other issues, turns a government into the street. The above-mentioned long Liberal régime in Quebec came to an end in this way; and the same thing was true of the fall of the Ross Government in Ontario early in 1905, following an unbroken Liberal administrative record extending back to Confederation. The Taschereau Government, by the way, would have gone out earlier but for an accident in which I played some part. The campaign of 1935 was nearing its close and the Government was facing defeat and knew it. I had occasion to make one of my periodical visits to that splendid lady, my mother, in Toronto, and while there I picked up a copy of the Toronto *Telegram*. It contained a dispatch from Washington asserting that advocates of the St. Lawrence Seaway in the United States were waiting for the Taschereau Government's defeat in order to press forward their project. I took this precious communication back with me to Montreal for reproduction in the *Gazette* and for editorial comment. The Liberal party became rejuvenated. The *Telegram* dispatch was seized upon and published throughout the Province. There is no doubt that it saved the Government for the time being. But in 1936 there were no accidents.

10

England and the English

I̶N THE otherwise agreeable month of June, 1924, I went to England on one of those holidays so keenly enjoyed by busmen. I was to relieve the Montreal *Gazette's* resident correspondent in London, who had married a wife, etc. It so happened that the Bar Associations of North America were being entertained by their bewigged British brethren, that the British Empire Exhibition was in progress at Wembley, that a special envoy of the Canadian Government was cavorting about on some mission or other, that the president of the Canadian Pacific Railway was in the vicinity, and that by and large the place was over-run with Canadians. The Dominion Minister of Finance was there, the late beloved Jim Robb of Huntingdon; Sir Lyman Duff was there, and there were, of course, the permanent agents and agencies of the Dominion and the provinces.

I had sublet from the resident correspondent aforesaid an ancient flat in Mitre Court, hard by one of those venerable inns where the original exponent of Johnsonian bad manners and abuse was wont to revile the shrinking Goldsmith in terms too faithfully recorded by the objectionable Boswell. This flat looked out on King's Bench Walk, where the beaux and belles of the eighteenth century and people who were neither belles nor beaus used to foregather for legitimate and other purposes. The most interesting thing about the place was the tradition that it, or the corresponding space, had been the home of Charles Lamb. The building was obviously very old, with interminable worn stone stairs that wound everlastingly upward to landings where were mighty doors of old oak, swung on enormous iron hinges and opened with keys of vast dimensions. Moreover, there was a cupboard in the flat converted out of what was said to have been Lamb's actual entrance and the door to this cupboard had an uncanny trick of swinging open without rhyme or reason, presumably to admit the ghost of Elia.

It is perhaps unnecessary to remind any experienced tripper that we rubbed elbows with Paper Buildings, Pump Court, the magnificent Middle Temple Hall, and the lovely Church of the Templars, where marble effigies of the Crusaders look for ever at a ceiling fully justifying their attention. And we were only a little way from Fountain Court, which Dickens knew and wrote about.

Furthermore, there was, or just had been, an old and bearded gentleman whose duty it was to stand at the entrance of the court after ten o'clock at night, the entrance being barred by a gigantic door of ponderous oak, studded with iron, and this gentleman had been Charles Dickens's office boy.

．　．　．　．　．　．

We went to Paris, crossing on one of those little channel steamers running from Folkestone to Boulogne, a notoriously evil experience for indifferent sailors, but the journey was made interesting as well as instructive by the uncanny ability of the stewards to arrive at the psychological moment with their enamelled equipment. They appeared to be engaged in a sort of joyous competition. Congregating at a strategic point, they would scan the decks expectantly. Suddenly one of them would become tense like a pointer. "There," he would say, "is one," and off he would go. "There is another" would come from a second steward and he would depart with undisguised enthusiasm. And so it would go on, a succession of races, and usually successful races, against time and eruption. I have known only one comparable example of professional pride. It was given by a humble but busy factotum in a hospital wherein I was once a patient. His name was Oscar and his heart was in his work.

My most dominant recollection of Paris, apart from the rapacity of its merchants, is of the great Church of Our Lady, that stupendous relic of mediæval magnificence. Notre Dame is to Paris what St. Paul's is to London, but it is older than the existing English cathedral and infinitely richer in a history that seems to be almost palpable. We stood before this majestic church, on ground where once a lovely and light-hearted Queen of Scotland was wed to a Dauphin of France. I looked up at the noble façade whose beauty has survived the ages, and I could almost see the terrible Quasimodo swinging a luckless scholar by the feet from a high gallery. I thought it not unlikely that we should hear the formidable hunchback crying, "Sanctuary, sanctuary," and reviling his pursuers.

We entered, and came out, impressed with a sense of the industry and genius of a bygone age, and of modern neglect. One does not attempt to describe so vast a miracle as Notre Dame de Paris.

It was a wet day. We found an inn on the lower side of the Seine and dined there, but there was some mistake about the wine. We were served with an enormous bottle, sufficient for five people, and it was good wine. I felt that none of it should be left. Later, and not long later, there was reason for a reversal of opinion.

I left Paris, without any of its inhabitants endeavouring to sell me postcards, and crossed to Dover, incidentally beholding the celebrated chalk so dear to the nostalgic heart of the English sailor coming home from "furrin" parts. We "did" the terrible old Tower, the National Gallery, St. Paul's and the Abbey, not as in duty bound, nor with the speed of an Indiana tourist, but in the satisfaction of an inherent hunger, an insistent craving that is in all English blood. I went to the old Abbey with Sir Lyman Duff, a most enlightened guide, and later I went again, to wander up and down, or sit a while in some quiet corner, soaking in the story of the greatest race the world has yet produced.

Some years ago, in an otherwise mediocre book, I came across the sentence, "England is greater than her people," and it is true in the sense that the race is deeply rooted, that it has back of it a great tradition and that, consciously or unconsciously, the long history of Britain is a blood content of every child born of British stock. Hence it is that in confronting any crisis, the individual Briton reacts to all that has gone before him and of which he is the product. There are extraordinary inconsistencies about these people. The most home-loving race in all the world has been the most adventurous, and the greatest colonizing force in history. Shakespeare's little island in its silver sea has become the centre of the mightiest Empire the world has ever known. A nation of shopkeepers has given leadership to all humanity in the science of government, in many of the other sciences and arts. But I have never been able to understand how these English—and I am an Englishman—acquired their reputation as a prosaic, unemotional and undemonstrative people. They are anything but that. They have glorified their institutions, their heroes, and have asserted their pride of race upon a scale unequalled by any other nation. They use the word "our" in speaking of Imperial possessions, of domestic customs, even of their industries, their cheeses and their sauces, as if there existed an actual personal partnership. They even look upon certain trade names and world-known labels as part of their inheritance and nobody can convince them that the products of any other country are or can be equal in quality with their own. We have always been asked to believe that the Englishman is not given to parade and circumstance in any of his activities and that in this respect he compares in some superior way with the volatile Frenchman. It is all a delusion and a humbug. In their state ritual the English are still doing what was done in chain-mail times, and in exactly the same way and with the same garb and trappings, merely because these things are English and, therefore, good.

One example may be cited to illustrate what I mean in saying that the English are not the reserved and inarticulate people they are represented as being. In the floor of Westminster Abbey, near the west entrance, rests the black marble slab which marks the tomb of the unknown soldier. It is the nation's tribute to the men who served and died in the ranks of the Great War and were buried in nameless graves in Flanders and in France, as well as in other fighting areas. Nothing can be said against this act of appreciation. It is as fine a thing as any country could do as a memorial. But this marble slab bears a very lengthy inscription: true, a very noble one, very rich in its phraseology, possibly a bit grandiloquent. It begins: "Beneath this stone rests the body of a British warrior, unknown by name or rank, brought from France to lie among the most illustrious of the land, . . ." There seems to me to be a little note of condescension here, and it jars. Surely this poor body came to the great Abbey as a matter of right and not of privilege, as being equal with "the most illustrious of the land"; yet even in a grave so glorious he must needs be the victim of a deeply-rooted snobbery. The inscription goes on, "and buried here on Armistice Day, 11 Nov., 1920, in the presence of His Majesty George V, his ministers of State, the chiefs of his forces, and a vast concourse of his nation. Thus are commemorated the many multitudes who during the Great War of 1914-1918 gave the most that man can give, life itself, for God, for King and Country, for loved ones, home and Empire, for the sacred cause of justice and the freedom of the world. They buried him among the kings because he had done good toward God and toward His house." Fine, sonorous lines, these, impressively majestic, but a trifle fruity, a shade ornate. The author—was he an ecclesiastic?—was just a bit garrulous and failed to observe the reputed English habit of reticence. And what of the noisy French? Under the mighty Arc de Triomphe which stands in the Place de l'Etoile where eleven avenues join that noble thoroughfare, the Champs-Elysées, there is another stone and under it the French "*Inconnu.*" And the legend is this: "*Ici repose un soldat français, mort pour la patrie,*" and a flame of fire burns there always and for ever. Personally, I think our French friends have much the best of the argument.

But no one who comes into contact with the Briton in his own stronghold can doubt that there is a reason for British domination of world affairs. Take the Londoner. He may not be either clever or smart in the New York or Chicago or San Francisco sense, but he is extraordinarily able. He does not talk about it and in this respect at least he justifies his reputation for reserve, but people are prone to forget that what they have been doing for a few generations and what they think they excel in

doing, the Londoner has been doing for hundreds of
years.   During my visit the English Bar, with the
help of the Canadian Bar Association, was, as I have
said, entertaining delegates of the American Bar
Association.   Now the Americans are no mean hosts
and most of these delegates went across the ocean
expecting to be accommodated and entertained
upon a standard inferior to their own.   Their eyes
were not only opened but kept open, alternately
staring and goggling.   There was no ostentation
anywhere, but there was a hospitality so generous,
so rich and comprehensive, that those who had come
prepared to be disappointed remained to marvel.
And the most disconcerting and puzzling element
in this demonstration of good will was the appearance of being spontaneous, a natural and normal
scale of reception.   The delegates from this side of
the water came away not sadder but certainly very
much wiser men, having about them an unfamiliar
quality of humility.

The English people are very good at pageants
and at Wembley they excelled themselves, more
especially in portraying the whole of the country's
long and colourful history down to Trafalgar.   I
cabled an extensive account of this performance,
obtaining my material from the official programme.
It so happened that I was a day or two in advance of
the event.   The regular London correspondents of
Canadian papers were immediately in receipt of
angry telegrams suggesting that they leave their
sleeping quarters and attend to their knitting.   Of
course, they replied that the pageant had yet to be
staged, but no telegraph editor has ever been
satisfied or even appeased by so obviously lame an

explanation. One of the victims came to me and remonstrated, though more in sorrow than in anger. I assured him that it was all a mistake and we went off to lunch at the National Liberal Club, where we admired the famous gorgonzola staircase.

In due time we left the great city, where the Englishmen, roaring after their prey, do seek their meat from Lyons, and made our way to Edinburgh and, of all the cities that I have seen, Auld Reekie has left its deepest mark upon me. I could make a hobby of Princes Street. If there is a thoroughfare anything like it I do not know where it is to be found. Its shops are as no other shops are, even its atmosphere is its own. The great castle frowns down upon it but Princes Street smiles back, serene and friendly as a Scottish girl might smile upon the man she loves. Nowhere in the world is there another setting equal to this, no gardens more gracious, no hills more rich in history. And a road leads down to Holyrood, that place of tragic memories, of shame and treachery and blood. The palace stands today much as it did in Mary's time, but the church beside it is a ruin. Perhaps it could not live in company with such a neighbour. And beyond is Arthur's Seat. Edinburgh and its environs are a great stage upon which have been enacted every sort of drama that ambition and passion and bigotry and sacrifice could inspire. The puppets have played their parts and have gone, but their ghosts are still about and I think will always be. I hope some day to go back to what is to me a city of enchantment.

11

Leaders and Misleaders

SIR ROBERT BORDEN
formed his Union or War Government in 1917,
again without the co-operation of Laurier, but with
the active help of other outstanding Liberals and the
support of a large body of Liberal opinion throughout the country. Again the Liberal element
became so influential under this new political
set-up—not by any means a novelty in Canada—
that Borden was more or less openly accused by
Conservative diehards of having ruined his party.
The charge was unwarranted, but even if it had
not been, Sir Robert would have been fully justified
in subordinating party fortunes to the main purpose
which the Dominion had in hand under his leadership. Subsequent events showed that he made a
wise step and that Conservatism as a political

element in Canada had not suffered. Much worse things have been done to it more recently. It was Sir Robert's resignation, rather than any party demoralization that made the Conservative Convention of 1927 necessary. Sir Robert relinquished his office, as was announced at the time, upon the advice of his physicians, but it was not generally known then, or since for that matter, how serious was the physical threat which forced his retirement. From what he told me it was plain that he had no alternative; had he remained in active leadership he could never have had the many years of tranquillity and civic usefulness which he actually enjoyed. He was a great lover of books and flowers and he spoke to me very feelingly of the happiness that was his in those later years in the company of his books or in the beauty of his garden at "Glensmere," things that he was never able to have as a lawyer in Halifax or as a political leader in Ottawa. He was very happy, very contented in these years of leisure.

Although there was some highly original idea of securing opinions from the rank and file of the Conservative party as to who should be Sir Robert's successor, and something of this kind was actually tried, the choice really lay between two ministers and two only, Sir Thomas White and Mr. Meighen. The former could have had the succession. As Minister of Finance he ranked next to the Prime Minister, he had been acting in Sir Robert's absence and he was the retiring chieftain's own choice, although Sir Robert's preference was never stated publicly so far as I know. There were several reasons for Sir Thomas' refusal. He was not

sufficiently rugged physically to withstand con-
tinuously the strain of public life and public office.
I am not sure that he ever had very much taste for
politics.   I do know that so long as he remained in
the Government he was making a very heavy
financial sacrifice.   He was without political ambition but content enough to disregard his personal
interests so long as he believed his services to be
necessary to the country's welfare.   But at this
time, with the war over, his greatest work was done
and he felt free to withdraw.   Furthermore, he was
strongly disinclined to enter into any contest for the
premiership, and it appeared that a contest of some
sort would be unavoidable.   He stepped aside and
the Borden mantle fell upon the Meighen shoulders.
In the circumstances it could have fallen nowhere
else.

It is an odd thing, by the way, that the highest
governmental office was always just a little beyond
the reach of the most experienced administrator in
the ranks of the Conservative party.   Sir George
Foster had served in the Macdonald, the Abbot, the
Thompson, the Bowell, the Tupper, and the Borden
governments, had served with consummate ability
in them all, and yet in all the changes that followed
the death of Sir John Macdonald the premiership
was never within his grasp.   There were reasons for
this, among them the fact that Foster was a thin
man, not physically only but intellectually as well,
at any rate until very late in his long life.   He had
been a schoolteacher and a university professor
and the atmosphere of the classroom seemed to
surround him always.   He neither drank nor
smoked—except perhaps a cigarette once in a while

in his later years at a press gallery dinner—and was an energetic temperance reformer. In appearance he was spikey and he had a bitter tongue. Where others chastized with whips, he punished with scorpions. He was the most incisive debater of his generation. He had been Minister of Finance and could discuss and manipulate statistics with apparent mastery, but he was never as much at home in building up as he was in tearing down. His forte was criticism rather than construction, and he used the acid unsparingly. He had been one of the nest of traitors in the Bowell Ministry.

As Minister of Finance he had been accused of starving the constituencies represented by his own party, and for this the party never forgave him. He had come almost—if not quite—unscathed out of the smelly business stirred up by an insurance commission in 1906, the matter of his investment of fraternal insurance funds while manager of the Union Trust Company. He even got some good out of this episode, because many people thought him the victim of political persecution and there was a reaction of sentiment in his favour. But his judgment, to say the least, had been proven faulty. That often occurs when the theorist tries to be practical. It happens also to the idealist in like circumstances and Foster's biographer has called him an "incorrigible idealist."[1]

He was a useful minister, a better oppositionist. Few ever thought of him as leader. But toward the end of his life he mellowed much and his disposition was sweetened. Furthermore, his sense of

[1] *The Memoirs of the Right Hon. Sir George Foster, P.C., G.C.M.G.,* by W. Stewart Wallace.

humour was acute and there was a glint behind the spectacles. His oratorical talent seemed to increase in range as he grew older, and the barbed wire minister of twenty or thirty years before became capable of deeply-moving, emotional reaches. One afternoon during the war, he rose in his place in the House of Commons and, obviously without pre-meditation, spoke of the conflict and its attendant suffering in accents so gentle and in terms so lofty and beautiful that none of those who heard, I am sure, have ever forgotten it. The Foster who died in 1931 was a very different and a much finer character than the sometime professor of classics and ancient literature whom Sir John Macdonald took into his cabinet in 1885.

The National Conservative Convention was held in the Amphitheatre in Winnipeg on October, 10, 11 and 12, 1927. That is to say, the general meetings were held there. It is probably true to say that most of the actual work was done in some rooms at the provincial parliament buildings or in others in the Royal Alexandra and Fort Garry hotels. I was there with the late Senator Smeaton White in the capacity of a delegate *ex-officio*, and I witnessed a great deal of the spade work. There was no doubt then that Honourable Howard Ferguson, Premier of Ontario, and afterwards Canadian High Commissioner in London, could have had the vacant leadership according to the temper of the delegates as they assembled for the first time in the Manitoba capital. There was equally no doubt that he could not have had it upon any terms after his rumpus with the Right Honour-able Arthur Meighen over the latter's memorable

Hamilton speech, in which he had laid down the policy that a war government should go to the polls and have its position endorsed directly by the people. Meighen chose the first day of the convention as the suitable occasion for an explanation of a position which he claimed had been misrepresented. He made his statement, apparently to the satisfaction of all the delegates present. Ferguson then took the platform and attacked the whole Hamilton proposition and, inferentially, its author also, with extraordinary vigour, but in the face of an obviously rising hostility. He was frequently interrupted and, although he succeeded in delivering his address, it was apparent that the rank and file of the convention were no longer with him. It was no less clearly evident that Meighen could have taken the leadership then and there had he wanted it. The curious thing was and is that neither man was willing to lead the federal Conservative party, yet both were willing to introduce a bitterly discordant note at the outset of the proceedings, indeed to set the whole convention by the ears. Neither one of them had anything to gain or lose by leaving the Hamilton incident alone. Meighen was determined, however, to clarify his Hamilton statement as a matter of principle, while Ferguson, as he afterwards explained to me, was equally determined to set forth the reasons for his own opposition to the Hamilton policy. He had threatened, or, let us say, promised Meighen that if the latter ever undertook to justify that policy he, Ferguson, would attack it. The opportunity came and he used it.

There was a vast deal of scurrying about, of group conferences and dismal discussions in hotel lobbies and elsewhere after this unhappy incident, and it was some time before the convention could get back to its feet.   Its main work was the selection of a leader, though it did pass upon certain questions of policy according to draft resolutions submitted to it.   Thirteen men were nominated, of whom seven withdrew.   Two ballots were taken, R. B. Bennett leading in both, though on the first he was 188 votes short of the total necessary for election. He had very little over the necessary quota on the second ballot, but it sufficed.   His speech of acceptance was characteristic.   In substance it was that he felt that he had been reserved for the service of his country, that he was a rich man and that his leadership would, therefore, be independent, and that he was prepared to devote all his talents and resources to the aforesaid service.   He spoke with his customary fluency and eloquence and the convention's cheers were loud and long.

Most of the delegates returned to their homes stimulated and satisfied; a few gave gloomy expression to their forebodings.   The convention had in fact chosen a leader possessed of great strength and great weaknesses, and, these qualities were curiously intermixed.   He was aggressive in Opposition and, in 1930, succeeded in carrying the country by a substantial majority of elected members.   What he failed to understand was that he was merely riding on the upswing of a political pendulum, that national electorates, in this as well as in other countries, had contracted a habit of alternating between one group and another, and that, in virtue of this political inconstancy, what goes up nearly always comes down.   Moreover, his promises, some of them, were incapable of fulfilment. The depression movement was still at or near its worst and the country had a long way to go. With all his very great ability, and with all his enormous capacity for industry, there were things which Mr. Bennett could not do. In addition, he made the mistake of constituting himself a one-man government. He was arbitrary, impatient of advice, and angry under criticism. He was given a great opportunity and, although he gave of his best unsparingly, he was far too temperamental to hold the loyalty of his colleagues as well as their obedience. It is sometimes just as bad politically to do a wrong thing as to do a right thing in a wrong way, but only a politician knows this, and R. B. Bennett never was a politician.

Pompous and dictatorial, he possessed as Prime Minister a genius for giving offence, even colleagues in his own ministry coming within the orbit of this unhappy talent. He endeavoured to be not only the head of the government but its torso and its limbs, and so completely did he centralize the administration of public affairs that other members of his government did not know where they were going, or why, in the development of party policy. The Winnipeg convention had laid down a platform. Mr. Bennett refashioned it to suit his own taste, and the rest of the government let him do it, while the Conservative representation in Parliament manifested a docility that was less an expression of deference to their leader than it was a revelation of invertebracy. Had the Conservative party, as represented in Parliament, shown the courage of its undoubted convictions and given Mr. Bennett an occasional piece of its mind, it might have made

something out of him. Its failure to do this was
just plain, ordinary cowardice, for which it paid.
Mr. Bennett had led the party up the hill, and its
members permitted him to lead them down again,
down to defeat and thence down to a condition of
impotence such as this traditionally great party
had never known in all its long history.

The Ottawa Agreements have been called Mr.
Bennett's greatest achievement. Men who were
very close to the proceedings of that conference
from day to day will tell you a very different story,
a story of explosive temperamentalism in the field of
diplomatic negotiation, and they will also say that
the conference very nearly failed. My own opinion
is that it did not fail because it could not. The
British ministers, Baldwin, Chamberlain, Hailsham,
Thomas and MacDonald could not have afforded
to go back to England empty-handed. Neither
could the Canadian Government have faced public
opinion in this country with the responsibility of
having wrecked an enterprise of such vital and far-
reaching importance to the Empire.

The fact is that nerves were not in good order
on either side. The British Government had been
strenuously busy, following the crisis of the previous
year, and their desire was to confine their activities
in Ottawa within as rigid business limits as possible.
Prior to their departure for Canada I had been
asked to suggest to the Canadian Government that
social functions be reduced to the lowest possible
minimum, and I had succeeded in securing the
Prime Minister's co-operation, which, of course,
carried with it that of his colleagues. It so happened
that by far the largest reception and entertainment

given during the conference was provided by the British delegates themselves. The point is, however, that these ministers from Downing Street were very tired men, and they found themselves obliged to do business with a Canadian as different in character and in conduct as there is space between the Poles.

I believed then and still do that the principal trouble so far as this country's case was concerned was a lack of adequate preparation. I had been warned well in advance of the Conference itself that something of this kind was in prospect. There were plenty of volunteer advisors on the ground when the conference assembled, but few of them were offering disinterested help. The London *Morning Post* at the beginning of May, 1932, had advocated the dispatch of official British experts to Ottawa at least a month before the conference to do the necessary spade work, as the North American Conference does in matters of shipping, and it might have been a very good thing if this suggestion had been followed, the Canadian Government having its own experts ready on the ground. Some of the more spectacular conference occurrences would probably have been avoided if this method had been pursued. Instead, the deliberations were conducted in a surcharged atmosphere and at times in a temper so unpleasant as to place the whole undertaking in jeopardy. Fortunately, the delegates had to come to terms. Alternate truculence and lachrymosity had to be overlooked if the whole business was not to be recorded in articles of failure. The result was nobody's achievement unless, perhaps, on the part of the British delegation, an achievement in patience, long suffering, and perseverance. Not that the results were disadvantageous to the Dominion. They were distinctly favourable, more so, in the opinion of British industrialists and exporters, than would have been the case if this country had afterwards observed what they considered to be the spirit, not to say the letter, of the Agreement. But Canada could have obtained just as much and still have had a reputation at Westminster for diplomatic dignity and governmental gentility.

.   .   .   .   .   .

At this writing, the summer of 1938, another Conservative Convention has just been held. I think I was responsible for it; at any rate, the first demand for a representative party gathering and a reconsideration of party policy was made by me in the editorial columns of the Montreal *Gazette*. But I am by no means proud of the outcome. There is no doubt in my own mind, as there is none, I know, in the minds of others, that in the organizing of this convention an attempt was made to defeat the party's main purpose, which was to get back to original Conservative principles and to proclaim them under new leadership. If Mr. Bennett's resignation announcement was made in good faith, and was intended to be kept, some of the things that happened at the convention are inexplicable. I believe that what he intended was a Bennett convention, one that would give him a renewed mandate which would permit him to exploit, in the name of the party and with its backing, the somewhat radical theories which he had espoused, and perhaps the still more extreme ideas, if they can be called ideas, expressed from time to time by his brother-in-law and alter egotist, Mr. William Herridge. I was not at the convention, but I do know something of what happened there, including Mr. Bennett's final discovery that he could not have the leadership, that if he entered the lists Dr. Manion would beat him. The nomination of M. A. MacPherson of Regina—who had not come East with any idea of competing for the leadership—was a manœuvre designed to bring about the defeat of Dr. Manion after it had become evident that the convention would not have Mr. Bennett. The trick failed, but if the spade-work had begun a little earlier it might have succeeded. Dr. Manion now finds himself leader of an as yet unorganized party and, I suspect, the object of one or two bitter enmities. Moreover, he stands upon a platform which is on the whole an expression of political cowardice.

In the first place the Resolutions Committee was hopelessly unwieldy. It developed into a debating society, and the discussions were more often acrimonious than judicial. The sub-committees were not much better, and the net result was that important declarations of policy were either watered down to innocuity or were frankly worded so as to conform to what the framers believe to be the lines of least political resistance. On the trade and tariff issues alone the platform is plain and understandable; but it has been a long time since that issue has meant anything as between the Conservative and Liberal parties, and it will not mean anything now unless the present Liberal

Government executes a complete surrender to its low tariff followers and thereby presents its opponents with the opportunity they need.

A friend of mine, after the Conservative platform had been published, said to me: "That is the end of the Conservative party." He is not a politician, but occupies a high place in industry. He may or may not be right, according to developments which cannot yet be foreseen. What genuine Conservatives hoped was that the convention would put the party back in its legitimate sphere, a sphere to the right of Liberalism rather than to the left where, under the Bennett leadership, it had been drifting. In the main the convention realized that hope.

The trouble is that there is very little room left to the right of Liberalism as practised by the King Government. For years the Liberal party has been doing what motorists call hogging the road. It has been moving along the crown of the highway, leaving the Conservative party no course but to fall in behind and sound its horn at intervals in ears that are conveniently deaf. Put it another way, the Conservative party has been stymied.

Many besides myself are thinking that conditions in this country will require ere long the formation of a strong non-partizan government, something on the lines of Sir Robert Borden's Union Ministry, a government enjoying a large measure of Conservative and Liberal support. Such a government will deal with major national problems in a way that, apparently, no partizan cabinet dare attempt. Its main work done, there may be, and I think there must be, a reshuffle, resulting in the formation of a Conservative party that will be conservative and

a Liberal party that will be liberal. Neither of
these new parties need be embarrassed by the
presence of conflicting elements such as those which
have brought the Dominion now into the curious
position of having two major political parties whose
names are virtually meaningless.

. . . . . .

Why did not the Right Honourable Arthur
Meighen accept the party leadership? He possessed all the requisite qualifications, more than
that, he had exclusive possession of them. People
have said that he is not a good politician, and they
have said the truth, but that is one more reason
contributing to his fitness not only for party
leadership but for national leadership at a time
when, because politics are paramount, the country
is undergoing a slow but steady process of strangula-
tion. The people of Canada must somehow get
above politics or politics will submerge and drown
them. The Conservative Convention failed to see
this; it played the old shoddy and shameful game
and never lifted its eyes to the heights. Senator
Meighen thinks upon a different plane, one which,
unhappily, the ordinary political mind cannot
reach. I don't know how strong was the pressure
exerted upon him from within the party, but I do
know that a tremendous effort was made to induce
him to accept the leadership and that it continued
almost up to the hour of voting. It was exerted in
the belief that Senator Meighen alone could give
the Dominion—not the Conservative party alone—
the guidance which, from some source or other, it
must obtain if it is to avoid or overcome the dangers

by which it is menaced in its domestic affairs and in its external relations.   Arthur Meighen's intellect has not its better in this country and perhaps not its peer.   His experience has been ample and his knowledge of national and international issues is profound.   If I am not wrong, his reluctance to undertake the labours and anxieties of leadership grew from his appreciation of the task's true magnitude, an appreciation of which far too many Canadians, including men prominent in public life, have shown themselves incapable.   But was his refusal justified upon that ground?   Were not the very reasons for his refusal the very reasons which should have compelled him to accept?   Only from a man who understands the nature of the service which this country required, and who, coupled with that knowledge, has a capacity commensurate with the collective gravity of the issues at stake, can the Dominion hope to secure the service necessary to its safety.   Had Senator Meighen in these circumstances a right to decline?   He had the power to decline, and exercised it, but, from the standpoint of civic responsibility and public duties, was any choice left to him?

Of course, it is very easy to present an argument of this kind and to lay down rules of conduct and set up standards of duty for other people's observance.   I have known Senator Meighen for thirty years, and fairly well, and in considering his attitude toward the leadership I am inclined, even in an atmosphere of disappointment, to concede the probability that he knew his own business best, that in this instance he weighed all the circumstances, all the political considerations—and some of these were of first-rate importance—and that he found himself the victim of circumstances where otherwise he might have been the servant of destiny. And he is at least as good a judge of his own responsibilities as any of those who have criticized his refusal can possibly be. I am certain that he would not have turned his back upon an opportunity in which he believed, or would have hesitated to accept a responsibility which, in the light of conditions known to him, some of them, perhaps, to him only, he felt himself competent to discharge.

The outcome of the convention, and subsequent events, have not been embarrassing to the Liberal party or its leader. William Lyon Mackenzie King is a two-compartment personality. He is emotional and he is crafty. It was the emotional side, his sympathy with the under-dog, that took him into politics, via the office of Deputy Minister of Labour, and on the road to his present eminence. His craft has kept him in that office or restored him to it.

In his days as a *Globe* reporter he held somewhat aloof from his colleagues, though I think this was not deliberate but rather the result of a temperamental difference. They tell one story about him, and I believe that, upon rare occasions of expansion, he tells it upon himself. Toronto newspapers were making much of the mysterious disappearance of a young woman. Armed with a description of the girl, King set forth from the *Globe* office in a spirit of high resolve. He would find her or perish in the attempt. The first day he had no luck, although he walked many miles of streets and gazed somewhat boldly into the faces of great numbers of pedestrians. But on the afternoon of the second day he came upon a young lady who seemed to fulfil the police description in all particulars. Approaching this damsel, the reporter invited her to accompany him. The female accepted, with suggestive alacrity, and in a few minutes, probably to her great surprise, found herself in the *Globe* office. King was explaining the triumphant issue of his search when the City Editor, a hard-boiled person, emerged from his sanctum. He looked at King and he looked at the girl. The latter he dismissed, curtly and decisively. To the future Prime Minister he said: "King, if you ever again bring a prostitute into this office you're fired."

As a politician Mackenzie King has proven to be a first-rate boxer but never a hard hitter. His footwork has been amazingly skilful. He will never deal with a major issue if he can avoid it and he will never accept responsibility if he can divert it to the shoulders of a Royal Commission, a judicial tribunal or some other scapegoat. He is never at a loss for words but he very, very seldom commits himself. He has been the Artful Dodger of Canadian public life for many years, and latterly it has become more and more difficult for colleagues or deputations of citizens to get at him with suggestions, or, having got at him, to extract a plain "yes" or "no" from him. He retires for extended periods to the fastness of his retreat at Kingsmere, and the Council waits until he is ready to come back. He has some principles, or rather some inherited constitutional antipathies, but on most questions he is capable of accommodating himself to the view that is politically most promising. Had it not been for this Gladstonian facility he could never have succeeded in holding the support of the Progressives and so continuing in office after the 1925 election with his party actually in a minority, although, for obvious reasons, there was a much narrower gap to bridge between Liberal and Progressive policies than between Conservative and Progressive.   Mr. King was skating over very thin ice at that time, and I question if any one but he could have displayed the same dexterity.   His campaign addresses are like those he delivers on the floor of the House, circumlocutional, and it takes a great deal of threshing to get at the kernel, when there is one.   Nevertheless Mr. King has an uncanny knack of sensing public opinion and the public themselves have turned to him repeatedly in the belief that they would enjoy greater tranquility under his administration than under one possibly more active and energetic.   He is extremely clever also in seeking out his opponent's most vulnerable points and concentrating his artillery upon those points.   He will not go down into history as a great leader or a great Prime Minister, but he most certainly will have provided for posterity an example of successful expediency. He has some noble personal qualities, a very kindly heart, and he is one of the rare men who do not permit political differences to interfere with personal relationships.

12

Short Inkpot Soliloquy

I WISH some sentimentally imaginative person could have the opportunity of communing with a pewter ink-well—it may be lead—a round squat receptacle, of which I am wrongfully possessed. These wells were standard equipment in the Green Chamber up to the commencement of the century and possibly for a little time thereafter, and, being virtually indestructible, they had continued in use from the days of the first Parliament. Now it was the practice to collect all the wells from time to time in baskets, presumably to clean them, and then to redistribute them among the members' desks so that it is at least possible, if not indeed probable, that the well reposing on my table was used at different times by all members of all the parliaments from 1867 up to the moment when it was, shall we say, acquired by myself. If we pursue this interesting theory or speculation, we can see the dipping of innumerable pens into this

218

little well, the pens of the greatest statesmen that have graced the halls of parliament in times gone by, the pens of the most corrupt politicians and the pens of the ordinary run of parliamentary representative whose principal mission has been to exemplify the traditional difficulty of converting sows' ears into silk purses. It is at any rate quite safe to say that with the ink out of this well were written many of the laws of the land, or, if not the bodies of the statutes, the alterations and amendments which they underwent in the often stormy course of their passage. It is not less safe to say that the dead hands which dipped their pens into this well wrote some of the great classical orations which have gone into parliamentary history and it is probably equally true that the same little object supplied the ink for communications of a highly secret and confidential sort, which no third person ever saw, but which altered the form and fate of governments. Because things like that have happened in our House of Commons, have happened many, many times, and the world knows only the bald results. There have also been critical occasions when the leader of a government has found it expedient to confer more or less in secret with the leader of the Opposition and this inkwell of which I am speaking may have supplied the cryptic message here reproduced.

The well, by the way, requires a certain amount of restoration. It has lost its original symmetry, having been thrown long ago at an amorous feline which was giving unmusical voice to its nocturnal social instincts. And the worst of it was that I missed the lecherous little beast altogether.

June 26.

my dear Borden,

can I see you
in my room at
one o'clock, or before,

Yours

Wilfrid Laurier

13

Union Without Unity

W E HAVE NOW REACHED
a stage in Canada when we must either solemnly
and honestly reaffirm the vows of 1867 or watch
while the whole Confederation structure comes
tumbling down. For a long time the process of
undermining the foundations has been in progress.
The Maritimes have never been satisfied with the
benefits accruing to them from the union, although
those benefits have been again and again extended
and enlarged. I asked a very prominent Nova
Scotian once, a former cabinet minister, what would
satisfy his province. His reply was in substance
this: "Nothing. Why should we be satisfied?"
There would be, of course, no possibility of coping
successfully with an attitude of that kind were it
typical. It is not a fair expression of eastern

sentiment or eastern sincerity. I have never found among fair-minded people in central Canada any disposition towards impatience with the Maritimes. Undoubtedly there has been indifference toward Maritime interest, but the responsibility for it must be placed upon the shoulders of the Dominion parliaments, up to, at least, the turn of the century. This is all the more curious in view of the fact that the provinces by the sea were loyally represented in the House and in successive cabinets. Their concerns were pleaded annually and vigorously on the floor of the House of Commons. Yet nothing of a broadly constructive nature was done until the appointment of the Duncan Commission in 1926 and while it is true that the recommendations of that Commission, and of other investigating bodies, were implemented in large measure, the fact remains that these provinces had to fight for everything that they got and that nothing was given them, virtually nothing, except upon the advice of third parties.

All this is not easily understandable having regard to the fact that all the Maritimes ever asked was justice, a fulfilment of the spirit as well as the letter of the Confederation pact. That their demands or requests, call them what you will, went unanswered for so many years is a serious reflection upon the legislative body which owes its existence to a movement originating in these very provinces. It has been an illustration of the federal habit to forget the rights and interests of the provincial units which made the Confederation and must be relied upon to maintain it, if it is to be maintained. The Honourable Fleming Blanchard McCurdy of Halifax, a very experienced and capable parliamentarian, and one who had held important governmental offices, went out of public life five or six years before the appointment of the Duncan Commission, having reached the conclusion that it was impossible to serve the Maritime Provinces as they should be served. The country thus lost from its councils one of the best informed and ablest of its eastern citizens, a man of wide influence and interest in his native Province of Nova Scotia. McCurdy had entered Parliament in 1911 under the most promising auspices, having defeated no less a person than the Honourable W. S. Fielding in Shelburne and Queen's, where Laurier's Finance Minister had ruled supreme for fifteen years.

But all the real or fancied troubles or grievances of the Maritimes and the disturbances that they have caused have dropped into insignificance by reason of more recent developments in the great central and western provinces, in Quebec, in Ontario, and on the prairie. British Columbia alone seems to be minding its own business. Alberta has frankly gone crazy and Saskatchewan has very narrowly escaped a similar fate, with Manitoba ready to throw in its lot with its two western neighbours if it becomes a choice of swimming with the stream or attempting to stand against it.

In a general way it is not difficult to explain the uprise of Social Credit in Alberta. The most westerly of the Prairie Provinces had, in common with its neighbours, suffered a long visitation of economic adversity, but in Alberta the popular spirit did not show the same resilience as in Saskatchewan and Manitoba, possibly because of a difference in main racial origins. Agriculture was said to have collapsed and those engaged in it had undoubtedly been buffeted by one reversal after another. Unemployment was widespread and the Government, even with liberal assistance from Ottawa, was unable to make ends meet. The general sentiment was one of despondency born of defeat. It is significant that, notwithstanding the occasional speeches of Messrs. Irvine and Spencer, as late as 1934, Social Credit had not become an issue in the province, and it is probably safe to say that seventy-five per cent. of the people had never considered it.

The seed was sown, or at any rate watered, in 1935, by Mr. William Aberhart, a Calgary High School principal who also conducted a religious establishment known as the Prophetic Bible Institute. Aberhart was born in Ontario of German and English parentage, the German father having lived all his life in this country from his childhood. Aberhart literally "preached" Social Credit, using the pulpit of his institute to proclaim and, up to a point, explain his economic theory, and throughout the campaign of 1935 his political appeals had a strong evangelical flavour. Indeed, he would alternate between one theme and another, between the practical and the spiritual, at intervals during the same address. Bear in mind that he was speaking to a disheartened population, a population which included a great many foreigners; also that he was promising regular monthly dividends payable out of the resources of the province. He made extraordinary headway, being gifted with a power of impressing his hearers, often enough against their judgment. This has been acknowledged by men who scouted his theory and were wholeheartedly antagonistic to the man.

Major C. H. Douglas, the father of Social Credit, had come to Canada in May, 1935, as reconstruction adviser to the Reid (United Farmer) Government and had presented an interim report on the possibilities of applying Social Credit principles to the province, recommending what may be described as a gradual approach to the employment of his theory. Douglas, it will be recalled, also advised the Aberhart Government but in no very enthusiastic terms, and eventually Mr. Aberhart was left to his own peculiar pursuits. Douglas himself, in tracing the Social Credit movement in Alberta, speaks of the economic difficulties which existed and of the people's distress. He describes Aberhart as a spellbinder, says that he or some of his advisers possessed an almost uncanny political sense and instinct, but that the Premier himself adopted a somewhat unfortunate policy after his election. He is confident, he writes, that it was not Mr. Aberhart's economics which carried him into office, "but rather his vivid presentation of the general lunacy responsible for the grinding poverty so common in a province of abounding riches, superimposed upon his peculiar theological reputation."[1] This I think is true. It is at least certain that those who voted for Social Credit, in 1935, responded to a promise rather than to their own understanding of a theory which Aberhart himself had failed to grasp. In short, the Social Credit election was an attempt by a despairing people to lift themselves out of their misery by the only device that was offered them.

[1] C. H. Douglas, *The Alberta Experiment.*

The Social Credit Government has not practised Social Credit, but it cannot be accused of lack of effort. Nor can it be accused of having done nothing for the people of the province. Some of its methods have been questionable, some of its enterprises have failed, but in several important instances the citizens' lot has been bettered, particularly in Mr. Aberhart's own professional field, that of education.

Ontario and Quebec for reasons of their own, and some of their reasons are sound, are openly and aggressively resisting what they profess to regard as a trend towards centralization, and this resistance is a very serious matter. The sum of all this is a weakening and loosening of the Confederation fabric. My own opinion is that the Dominion has been largely at fault. The Macdonald conception of federal responsibility has always prevailed at Ottawa and the history of Confederation has been a record of contests between the Dominion and this or that province over matters of legislative jurisdiction. In the majority of instances I think it can be said that federal encroachments, or attempted encroachments, have been responsible for these struggles and, unfortunately, the federal appetite for provincial rights has not been dulled by repeated rebuffs at the hands of the Judicial Committee in London. On the contrary, it has become more keen, and there has developed a very real danger of centralization arising from the fact that the provinces are too poor to finance the eleemosynary services which have come to be regarded as social and economic necessities. The federal authority, notwithstanding the manner in which it has squandered the country's resources, still has the money to provide these services, or can get it, and the provinces are confronted with the temptation of being able to spend millions of dollars annually from the federal treasury on enterprises which should be their own responsibility. As they take the money they relinquish their own authority, but in every politician or group of politicians—and no provincial government is anything more than a political group—the spending passion is overmastering. The whole situation has become so delicate that it is growing doubtful if Confederation can be saved by anything less than a non-partizan government. The Royal Commission, which has been investigating federal provincial relations, was weak at the beginning and lost caste more or less with the enforced retirement of its chairman. Two provinces have rejected its offices. Its findings are unlikely to be of any value, partly because of a general lack of confidence in the Commission's surviving personnel and partly because the sinister developments of which I have written are running too fast to be arrested by any Royal Commission, however strong. The future is very much in the lap of the gods and the only hope worth expression here is that they are not the gods whom so many people in this country in recent years have turned aside to worship.

It is trite and profitless to say that this is a difficult country to govern, that the interests of one part are in conflict with those of another, and so on. Of course these things are true, but no intelligent effort has ever been made since 1867, so far as I am aware, to find a remedy, much less to apply it. Canada will always be difficult to govern and sectional hostilities will continue to hamper and embarrass so long as the government itself is based on sectionalism. There can never be a mutual understanding where there is mutual ignorance, and ignorance rather than indifference to one another's problems is what is wrong with Canada, what lies at the bottom of the so-called struggle between the West and the East. Undoubtedly there is selfishness wherever a sectional interest exists, and equally certain is the fact that politicians, who should be builders, conciliators and welders, play upon such selfishness for their own purposes and aggravate ills in the body politic which it is their duty to heal. The way to mutual understanding and respect lies through the cultivation of mutual knowledge, and that field has been left untilled so far as any organized effort is concerned. But the faults of this generation and its predecessors need not be repeated in the one now rising, into whose hands the affairs of the Dominion must be in due time entrusted. The younger Canadians should be educated to the great task that lies before them, and it is still a sound principle to begin with them while they are young.

14

This Canada

IT HAS ALWAYS SEEMED TO me that a knowledge of his own country—or hers—should be an essential part of the education of every Canadian child. This could be undertaken only as a state enterprise and even then would involve serious practical difficulties. Nevertheless, with the co-operation of the companies operating our more than sufficient railways, the thing could be done, and its advantages would be incalculable. New generations of Canadians cannot be expected to understand and deal with the problems of a country which they do not know. It is a grand country. There is no other like it, or at any rate, none equal to it, whether in territorial extent or in the variety and richness of its beauty, the diversity and abundance of its resources. The late Canon Tucker

229

of London, Ont., once preached in my hearing an unforgettable sermon in which he ranged the wide world for examples of scenic splendour, and found their counterparts in Canada.   There is something deeply impressive even in the iron desolation of the Labrador coast, or of what was once so called. There is magnificence beyond expression in the stupendous cathedrals of rock upflung to the sun and to the stars in the far west.   The eye finds rest and the soul refreshment in the endless green or gold of the prairies, Bryant's gardens of the desert. You can find in the interior valleys of Nova Scotia, if you will, everything that has given the English countryside its everlasting fame.   You can find Scotland in Canada, and Ireland and Old France, if you care to seek them and have eyes to see.   Have you ever come in to the Gaspé coast at Percé in the moonlight, from the sea?   Have you ever seen a full-rigged sailing ship passing up the Bay de Chaleur, its great spread of canvas throwing back the changing colours of a setting sun?   Do you know the Malahat Drive on Vancouver Island, or the road down the Matapedia Valley in eastern Quebec? or anything of northern Alberta—the Last Great West —and what has been happening there in this generation?   Have you gone across the vast wilderness of northern Quebec and Ontario, or driven into that world of magic which is the Turner Valley, or rambled through the little garden province, Prince Edward Island?   Certainly a great and wonderful country—and far too little known.

I doubt if there is to be had anywhere else under the sun a season equal to Canada's autumn, the weeks just prior to and after Thanksgiving Day.

It does not mean much to the city dweller, to the man who cannot or will not leave the sidewalks. But to the man who lives in, or visits, the country there is in these autumn days a joy past all expression, a feast for the eye and mind, a great and solemn solace to the soul. Go, if you can, where there are hills and waters. Make your way by quiet roads and take your time in the going. Here is nature in her grandest raiment. She wears it only for a little while; a week or two and all the glory is gone and the bare branches tell of a dying year, but for this little time the world about is radiant, a superb panorama of red and gold and green, and every red has its thousand shades, every gold its flaming variants, every green its multitude of tints. And there is no order about them, only a bewilderment of beauty. The greatest of all painters has gone over the hills and down into the valleys with a master brush. Blue waters take down into their depths the splendour of God's colouring, and over all and upon all shines the soft autumn sun as if bathing the rich banners of an endless marching army. The season, too, has its own scents, and the air is full of them. In England, I believe, they call this time the crown of the year, surely a better and more fitting term than ours. And yet, "the fall of the year" is accurate enough, for the end is drawing near. The gorgeous garments of autumn will have been put off for winter's pure white robe of sleep, but no one should miss the autumn pageant while it is there to see. No one, above all, should fail to look, and look long upon the swiftly changing myriad colours of an October countryside under the magical mutation of a sun going down. The cattle are coming home then. The blue smoke mounts lazily from the chimney of a far-off farm. It is all indelible, and unforgettable. And autumn is only one season out of four, and each has its own beauty, its own message, each offers us something that is without money and without price, because it is beyond either.

Early in the rural or semi-rural period of my upbringing I looked from an upper window of a farmhouse and saw a June orchard with rain falling over it. I can see it now, and seeing can feel the same sensation that moved me so profoundly then, that of being present at one of nature's ancient rites, of witnessing a vital process, even an intimacy that I was not meant to see. That orchard has never left me, nor that rain. I was in one of life's secret places. How many of us, in springtime, look upon the furrowed field or the grass meadow under the melting snows, the showers and the sun, and have eyes to see? Yet this is nature in her bridal time, anon to be followed with the glory and the pride of motherhood. Then come the long fair days of summer, its whispering, languorous nights, and then the harvest—fruition—the old earth in her travail— the eternal mystery of procreation. Do the waving seas of green and yellow corn mean nothing to us but fodder for the beasts? Can we find no message, no evidence of an eternal truth, in the acres of tossing grain, in the full gardens, or in the twisted fruit trees, heavy with their yield? To the economist it is new wealth, but it is infinitely more; it is new life and the assurance of continuing life. All this we see go on from year to year, and yet we do not see it, unless perhaps in terms of money and of profits, and in those terms are expressed man's unworthiness of a glorious environment and heritage. The book of knowledge is open there before him, and he will not stop to read.

·   ·   ·   ·   ·   ·

I am bringing these rambling reminiscences to a close and with a melancholy reflection. It is that of any man of threescore years who, looking back over his adult life, sees the outward procession of so many men who were his friends. Where have they gone and what has become of all that they learned, each in his life's experience? Has it all been lost and wasted, and has this been going on through all the ages since man first reached his capacity to think and to build? I put this question to a learned friend of mine some years ago, an eminent lawyer, a cripple and a great sufferer. "Isn't that," he replied, "an argument for immortality?" I could not see it then and cannot see it now. It is all part of the great mystery which we are told man is not meant to understand. We live, and love and labour and we die, and we have no means of knowing what, if anything, has been, or is to be, the enduring fruit of our long effort. There is abundant foundation for the belief in a Creator. Faith in a redeemer rests upon certain historical facts if we are to accept the authenticity of the New Testament, but Christianity is possible even without such acceptance because it is an ideal of clean living which appeals to the best that man has in him, and the rise and spread of Christianity is, therefore, some proof of man's inherent desire to live decently with his fellows. Otherwise the thesis of Jesus Christ could

not have survived the persecutions which at the
outset were inflicted upon those who believed in it,
could not have survived the personal examples of so
many who have since professed it, could not have
come down through the ages with all its original
purity to supplant the Mosaic Law which is its
antithesis. It satisfies an instinctive longing, a
hunger that is present in every human soul and
which is the foundation of faith. If there is no
other foundation, none that can be expressed in a
syllogism of logic, it is because the mental range of
mankind is so limited and circumscribed. The
mind, which is essentially finite and ephemeral,
cannot grasp the things that are infinite and eternal.
Human understanding, which consists of the capacity to create mental images, is helpless in the
presence of those two words, "infinity" and
"eternity." Man, in his intellectual littleness,
must have some yardstick with which to find a
beginning and an end, with which to calculate a
dimension, if it be only in abstract terms; but
eternity has had no beginning and will have no end,
and infinity knows no dimension. We must perforce
have faith since we cannot reason, or, at any rate,
cannot complete our reasoning. We do know,
somehow, that beauty is everlasting and that truth
can never die, and in that knowledge our faith is
fortified. In virtue of that knowledge, and the
faith begotten of it, we go forward through life's
several stages, striving and achieving, blundering
and building, looking always to some distant star,
and with that armour on us we go forth at last, each
to his Valhalla, obeying the imperious gesture of
that arbiter who brooks no disobedience. For

myself, when the time comes, as it has come to all these others, I should like to think that I can take with me into that other country some memory of earth's green places, some recollection of the melodies that I have heard, some lingering echo of the singing of the sea.

Date Due

CAT. NO. 23 233   PRINTED IN U.S.A.

CPSIA information can be obtained
at www.ICGtesting.com
Printed in the USA
LVHW080006010522
717630LV00010B/628

9 781013 480492